THE MANDALA WAY

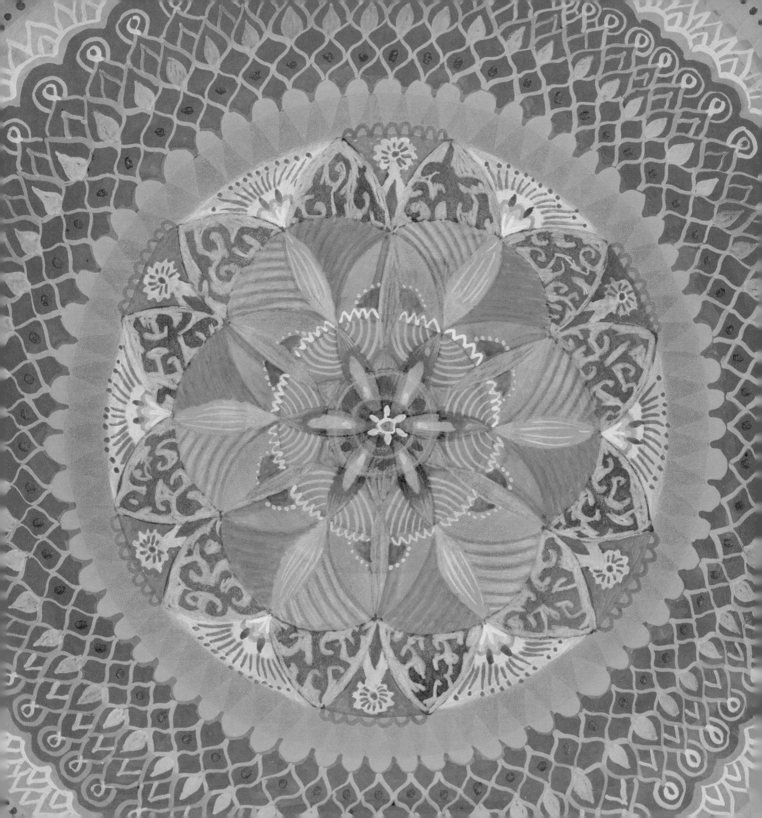

THE MANDALA WAY

A CREATIVE JOURNEY INTO HEALING AND SELF-EMPOWERMENT

Written and illustrated by
EITAN KEDMY

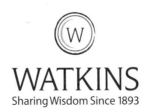

WATKINS
Sharing Wisdom Since 1893

The Mandala Way
Written and illustrated by Eitan Kedmy
Translated by Judith Erel

First published in the UK and USA in 2023 by
Watkins, an imprint of Watkins Media Limited
Unit 11, Shepperton House, 83–93 Shepperton Road
London N1 3DF

enquiries@watkinspublishing.com

Publisher: Fiona Robertson
Assistant Editor: Brittany Willis
Design concept: Kate Cromwell
Designer: Steve Williamson
Production: Uzma Taj

A CIP record for this book is available from the British Library

ISBN: 978-1-78678-716-3 (Paperback)
ISBN: 978-1-78678-728-6 (eBook)

1 3 5 7 9 10 8 6 4 2

Typeset by JCS Publishing Services Ltd

Printed in Malaysia

www.watkinspublishing.com

ACKNOWLEDGEMENTS

Heartfelt thanks to Ruth Dekel for her help in writing the original text and collecting the material; Jenny Rosenfeld for editing; Anat Rotem for documenting the lessons; Emma Ayalon for her insightful comments; my sister Edna for her support; my brother Yossi for his encouragement; my mother and father, of blessed memory; my daughters Alma and Kaya for being part of my life; Carl Jung, who opened the gateway; and all my students who have joined me on the mandala way.

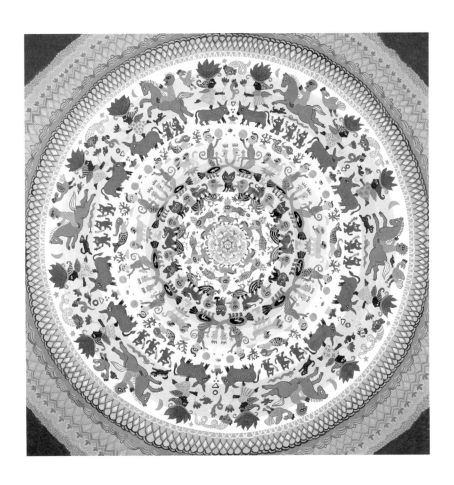

CONTENTS

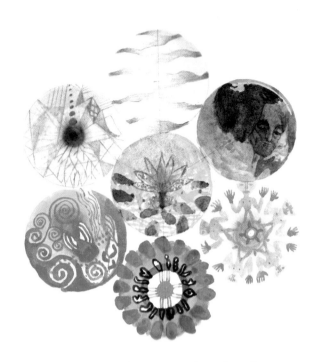

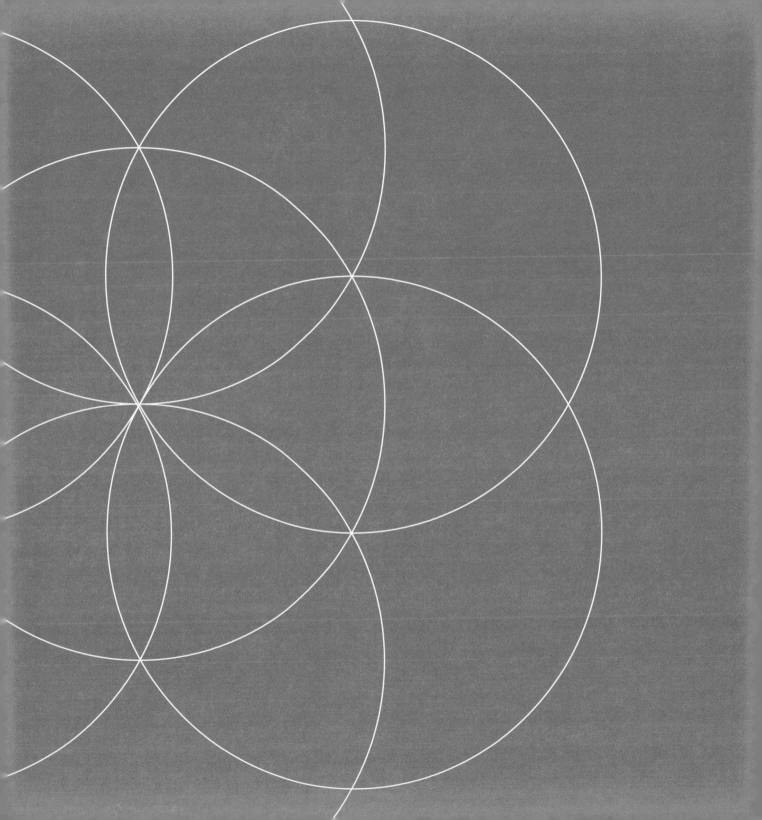

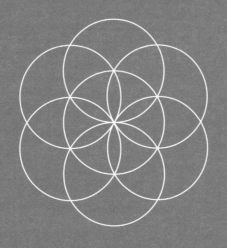

PART ONE
ABOUT THE MANDALA

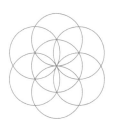

CHAPTER 1

WHAT IS THE MANDALA WAY?

The mandala way is a journey of self-discovery through creativity, expanded awareness and spiritual growth. The process of creating a mandala puts us into direct touch with our emotions, which speak to us in a language of colours and images, like in a dream. If we understand this language, it can open hidden windows to the depths of the soul and become a catalyst for generating change in our lives.

Drawing a mandala is, first of all, an enjoyable and relaxing activity. While we are working, the tempo of our life momentarily slows down and we experience a sense of inner presence. Creating a mandala deepens awareness, improves our ability to listen and concentrate, and enhances our feelings of self-worth and self-confidence. Through the mandala we can experience our "true self" and connect to our individual purpose.

A mandala is a creation in circles, beginning at the centre point and expanding outward. We look into our mind's eye and, using our imagination, give expression to the complex structure of our inner world of thoughts, feelings and experiences. Drawing mandalas connects us to our unconscious and helps us transform our dreams into focused goals that can be achieved.

The mandala way is a tool for spiritual development that helps us to know ourselves through the heart rather than through the mind. Like practicing meditation, drawing a mandala develops our ability to listen to our inner self and to come "home" to that inner place of comfort where we contain and accept ourselves with unconditional love. When we are "at home" – connected to the divine centre within – we feel a connection to the world. Life becomes easier and flows without a struggle. We are quiet and tranquil, free of worrisome thoughts and filled with positive emotions. When we dwell in our inner circle, we feel safe. We allow ourselves to slow down because we know that there is no destination. Life is here and now. There is no longer a need to yearn for the past or to fear the future. When we dwell in the home of the soul, connected to our centre, in our true essence, the gateways open and abundance flows to us effortlessly. We can stop searching because things come to us at exactly the right time and in the right amount.

The Mishnah (Jewish Oral Law, Tractate Ta'anit), tells of a year of drought in the 1st century BC. A righteous man of that time, Choni HaMe'agel, was asked to pray for rain. He drew a circle around himself and took an oath not to leave the circle until rain fell. After his prayers, rain poured from the skies. The mandala that Choni drew designated his connection to his own inner essence. When we have complete faith, then we have direct communication with the higher worlds that generate reality. Choni HaMe'agel symbolizes the ability to unite our inner world with the outer world.

In its essence, the mandala way is very simple. All we have to do is draw a circle, contemplate it, sketch a template within it and work from the circle's centre. This simple act directs the soul to embrace itself. The circle arouses a feeling of being enveloped in compassion. The love and compassion that we feel within the circle illuminates our inner essence and reveals the compass that directs us along the right path of our lives at every moment. In our inner essence, we discover clarity and knowledge about the next step that we should take. Through the mandala we can look at the mirror of the soul and listen to the heart's whisperings. We can ask questions, receive answers and find creative responses for unravelling complex problems. When our soul is in its home, we discover healing powers we never knew existed. By drawing the mandala we can immerse ourselves in pure spring water and be cleansed of the fears and false beliefs that we carry inside.

The Mandala Way was written so that anyone can use the simple power of the mandala – men, women, children, adults, those artistically inclined and those who have never held a pencil. There are 16 lessons that act as gateways to the rich, multi-dimensional world of the mandala. In the first eight lessons we learn to use basic patterns or templates such as the circle, triangle, square, spiral and so on. This prepares us for the next eight lessons, in which we embark on a personal journey through the body's energy system of chakras. All 16 lessons focus on a different and unique mandala pattern. Each mandala comes from a different cultural source and each template relates to a different aspect of healing and self-understanding.

The need and desire to draw mandalas is not accidental. Many mandala artists speak of starting to draw mandalas at a time of confusion, chaos and emotional distress. Drawing mandalas brought them new understandings and insights regarding the possibility of rebuilding and reorganizing their lives, like a death and rebirth. The mandala comes to us when we need it – either to reorganize our inner order or to open us up to new, unfamiliar experiences. If you are reading this book, it seems that the time has come for you to try the healing power of the mandala.

To get the most out of your mandala journey, first equip yourself with fine art materials: thick, good-quality paper, coloured pencils, a fixable compass, regular pencils and a ruler. Set aside time during the week to work quietly for at least an hour without outside distractions. Choose a well-lit space to work in, light a scented candle and play soothing music. Each mandala has a special meditation as inspiration for painting. Read the meditation, close your eyes and take three deep breaths. Once you have opened your eyes and feel ready and focused, start drawing the pattern.

My Personal Journey to the Mandala

When I try to recall the path I travelled prior to discovering the mandala, the first memory of note is my insatiable desire to draw and paint. I can't remember myself ever without paints and a paintbrush. In childhood I felt a strong need to observe nature. I would look for hours at flowers, ant hills, the cloud-filled sky or the froth of the sea's waves and then express these rapturous sights in paintings. I was a dreamy child who preferred looking in a microscope to playing football with the neighbourhood kids.

There was not much appreciation for art in my parents' house. Professions with status and power were much more valued. My mother's dream was that I become a medical doctor; my father preferred that I become a division commander. The option that I would become an artist was quite problematic.

I began my artistic exploration of circles with an exhibition at the Horace Richter Gallery in Old Jaffa. Horace, with his impressive mane of white hair, loved my sculptures from first sight and invited me to show them at his gallery. Most of the works were circles of figures around a centre.

"Charon's Circle" was a circle of male sculptures on a bed of coarse salt. Charon, a figure from Greek mythology, diligently performed his task of transporting the souls of the dead across the River Styx, which separated the world of the living from the world of Hades, god of the underworld. For some reason, ever since childhood, I had felt an affinity to this strange ferryman. He was close-mouthed, ornery, and feared by everyone. The ancient Greeks placed a coin in the mouth of their dead as Charon's payment in return for a safe trip across the Styx. In this work, a circle of male figures stand around the figure of Charon, symbolized by a white boat.

After the exhibition at the Horace Richter Gallery, I realized that my art did not stand on its own merits; it was just part of my personal healing process. A lack of peace and quiet again disturbed me. I knew I had to continue my search, but I had no map or compass to guide me. The message I kept receiving was that people in the world were going through a period of change and that it was necessary to separate from the old in order to reach the new. But how could you do this? The fear of change continued to reverberate within me. I felt as if I were drowning in a stormy sea. I didn't have the emotional strength to believe that something new would actually happen. Slowly I sank into a black hole with no point of return. It seemed as if I had reached the end of the road, with nothing connecting me to life. Everything was in a thick fog with no meaning. I refused the message that kept knocking on my door, to let go of the familiar and let something new grow. These were days of being lost, of not knowing where I came from or where I was going.

That was the very moment that the mandala entered my life. It appeared before me at a specific moment and without any notice. Drawing the mandala opened a new path of inner unity for me. I felt all the pieces inside me connect into one entity. My way was clear and all the questions were answered.

Each time I create a mandala I imagine myself as a child learning how to draw for the first time. There is no place for criticism when creating a mandala, only love and acceptance. The theory of psychoanalyst and philosopher Carl Jung introduced me to the collective unconscious. I connected to the healing power of man's creativity in all cultures. I became open to the treasure chest inside me, extracting ancient prayer beads, legendary creatures and mythological figures that know how to speak and fly through time.

I had discovered the reason man was endowed with the power of artistic creation: to heal the body and soul, to help the soul find its true purpose and to encourage people to create from a place of passion and vitality. The artist who heals recognizes his power and humbly knows his value. He knows that life is renewed at each moment – here and now. And at that moment everyone is equal and everyone is whole – just as they are. Artists who are in touch with their healing powers can awaken others to their own love and passion for life and direct them to the thin line between the soul and the unity of the universe.

My first mandala, created in 2004.
Blue plastic paint on an old phonograph
record covered with a white base coat.

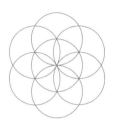

CHAPTER 2
WHAT IS A MANDALA?

A mandala is a representation of the external world in a circular pattern with a central point; a microcosm of nature, the planet earth, the solar system and the universe from the human perspective. In the same way, for someone drawing a mandala, it can be seen as a microcosm that mirrors or symbolizes the complex structure of his inner, spiritual and psychological worlds.

The word "mandala" is an ancient Indian Sanskrit word that means circle, describing anything whose shape is round. It is composed of two words: "Manda", which means "place that is high or raised above and of great value", and "la", which means completion, or the closing of a circle or cycle. The combination of the two words creates "a circle that contains the essence" and, as such, the mandala seeks to be a place that is sacred and pure. The pure essence that the circle envelops is hidden in the centre of the circle and, in Sanskrit, is called bindu: the point of divinity. The bindu is a peep hole between the revealed world and the hidden world.

According to the Kabbalah (a body of mystical teachings of rabbinic origin), the Hebrew letter yod (é) is analogous to the bindu and means "the point in the heart".

A Journey of Growth and Development

The fertilized egg, the eye and the womb are mandala-shaped organs that influence our development as humans and our perception of the world.

The human body begins its journey as a fertilized egg developing within the womb, a tiny bindu point that grows to become a complete person. The basic feelings and memories common to all humans are related to our once being fetuses protected within a round space, with a sense of unity with the mother's body and the entire universe.

Our bodies are built from cells which themselves are like a mandala, with a point, the nucleus, at its centre. Our eyes, too, are built in the shape of a sphere. Light rays pass into the eye cavity through the round pupil, and are carried by the optic nerves to our brains as a round picture. The mandalic experience is one of the first sensations we experience in life: as newborns, we burst into the world and search for the mandala-shaped breast to suckle.

Research has shown that infants prefer round shapes. This is a part of a newborn's survival instinct, which facilitates the identification of their mother's face. In the first period of life, when an infant lies helplessly on their back, gazing at the world, spatial perception is mandala-shaped, with the tip of the nose as the bindu, the only fixed point. The child perceives themselves as the centre of the world, like a bindu, with ever-widening social circles – parents, family members, neighbours and friends.

Children naturally draw mandalas as part of their cognitive and motor development. Their first doodles, in repetitive, circular motions, look like spiral mandalas. As their fine motor skills improve, they can draw a complete circle. Afterwards we see that they add other marks – the eyes, nose, mouth, hands and feet – to the circle.

Many idioms include the word "circle" (or its derivative, "cycle") to express a feeling of belonging, or of repeated patterns, such as: the family circle, a circle of friends, the circle of life, the yearly cycle, closing the circle and so on.

Describing Structure in the Universe

Humans conceived of the idea that the world is built of circles, almost from the moment we tasted the fruit from the tree of knowledge and began to investigate the essence of the world around us. The curving horizon line taught us that the earth on which we stood was circular. The primeval vision of the sun shining over the kingdom of the day and the bright moon lighting the kingdom of the night is at the heart of our perception of the universe. We are born onto a planet spinning on its axis, revolving around the sun as the moon rotates around us, creating cycles of time: day and night, weeks, months, years.

Nature is a source of infinite mandala images: flowers, birds' nests, tree trunks and water crystals, to name a few. The ripples that form when a stone is thrown into a lake is a wonderful image of the process of creating a mandala. The stone represents the bindu that creates the first ripple, out of which the next ripple is formed, and so on. Energy creates energy in a circular form. Creating a mandala is done in exactly the same way. The mandala originates at the bindu point; from that point an infinite number of ever-widening circles begin to form around it. In creating a mandala, we go from stage to stage without planning how the next stage will look. Starting to create a mandala at the bindu point is like removing a stone from the mouth of a spring, enabling the hidden waves of creativity in the unconscious to flow forth into the light.

Creating circles that alternately open and close, we become cognizant of the secret of the cycles of life, the rhythm of the breath, night and day. We cannot begin a new circle until we complete the previous one. When we give our complete attention to creating the circle, we develop a sense of wholeness and self-acceptance. Creating the mandala becomes an end in itself. Total presence and complete attention to the process fills the soul with tranquility. The mandala enables us to feel our body from the inside and to become aware of our emotions. Through the mandala we can experience the present moment as if it will last forever, be present and widen our perception of reality at the point that makes it possible to break through the constraints of the rational brain.

Creating Mandalas Since the Beginning of Civilization

Our forebearers created circular forms. In the caves where early people dwelled, spiral and circular etchings have been found. In different places in the world, we have the remains from prehistoric times of large stones, called megaliths, sometimes found in stone circles, and presumably used for ritual purposes.

There is one such example here in Israel. The "Ghost Wheel" ("Galgal Refaim" in Hebrew) or "Mound of the Wild Cat" ("Rogum al Hiri" in Arabic) is located in the Golan Heights near the village of Moshav Yonatan. Researchers do not know the reason why, 5,000 years ago, the Golan dwellers placed more than 42,000 basalt rocks in mandala circles, although the hypothesis is that the mound of rocks was used as a site of tribal ritual worship.

The huge rock structure of Stonehenge in Wiltshire, England is also an example of a prehistoric stone mandala that was perhaps used for stargazing and as an expression of the year's cycles.

All ancient cultures had a connection to circles. In the temples to gods in ancient Egypt, there are structures based on basic geometrical forms, like the Star of David and the pentagonal star. These symbols are used to transmit esoteric knowledge and belong to what is called Sacred Geometry. An example is the decorative geometric forms found in the temple to the Egyptian sky god Horus.

The relation between healing and circles can be seen in the Greek temple built for the god of medicine, Asclepius, in the city of Pergamon, today located in Turkey. There is a round room in this temple where the sick were asked to sleep and to dream. The priests then used these dreams to determine the remedy for their illness.

Native Americans also used mandala paintings for healing and thanksgiving ceremonies. The Navajo nation, which resides in Arizona and parts of Utah, is today the largest of the Native American nations. The Navajo shaman would draw shapes on the ground that were considered to have powerful energy, using coloured sand and coloured powders produced from wood charcoal and flower pollen. These were primarily images from the plant and animal worlds, such as the coyote, the crow and corn. The sick person was laid down on the mandala to absorb the energies they were lacking. The sand paintings, in the form of mandalas, were created to restore the sick individual to inner harmony and harmony with the universe. The sick person did not create the mandala themselves; only those who had undergone special training could make it. During the ceremony, the sick person sat in the centre of the mandala while the mandala's creators sang special healing songs. At the end of the ceremony, the sand mandala was dismantled.

The mandala is an important symbol in Native American cultures. Shamans of the Sioux tribe from the Dakota region of North America created medicine wheels symbolizing the structure of the world and the four directions. Black symbolizes the west, where the entities of thunder, lightning and rain dwell. The north is white, representing the north wind. Red symbolizes the east, the source of light and where the morning star shines, bestowing the light of intelligence and wisdom. Yellow in the south designates the summer, the earth and blossoming. A bowl of tobacco dedicated to the Great Spirit, the source of the other spirits, is placed in the centre, symbolizing the central, vertical axis of the mandala. The other directions, colours and elements spring from this centre, which symbolizes the human heart and the centre of the universe. During the ceremony called Hanblecheyapi, or "Vision Quest", the tribe's medicine man spends several days alone on the top of a mountain where he engages in meditation, hoping to experience the unity of the universe. At the meditation site, a cross, 10m (33 feet) high and 10m (33 feet) long, is drawn on the ground. During the ceremony, the medicine man presents offerings to the spirits in a circular motion around the four ends of the cross. The circular motion designates the mandala and the centre point as the source of unity of the four directions.

In Central America, the Aztecs believed in many deities. The deity called Ōmeteōtl was considered the supreme creator deity, the single source of multiplicity in the world. Ōmeteōtl manifested in both a male and female form that were united in one entity in an act symbolizing marriage and fertility. This god's home is in the world's navel.

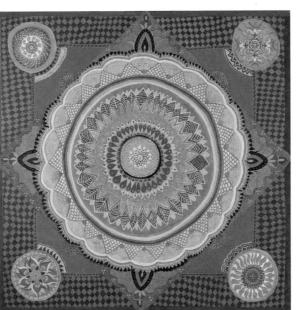

Celebration, created 2005.
Acrylic on canvas.

From there, the four directions issue forth, each one dedicated to one of his four sons. To each one of the sons is dedicated one of the four elements, colours and seasons of the year. The east, for example, is seen as a light, fertile area, associated with the colour red. In contrast, the north is cold, black and connected to death.

Aztec cosmology is also represented by a mandala shape. According to their belief, the surface of the world creates a very wide disc located at the centre of the universe. The disc has balanced, perpendicular extensions in the form of a cross that are surrounded by sky and water. The mandalas face in the direction that shows the sun's movement on the shortest and longest days of the year. It is thought that they were used as calendars denoting unity between time and place, and between humanity and the universe.

The Aborigines, the indigenous population of Australia, considered to be the oldest continuous living culture on earth, made drawings that expressed an object's essence by connecting circles and dots. In this way they recounted the Aboriginal mythology called "dream time", which depicts the creation of the world and humanity's connection to nature.

Especially mysterious and fascinating are "crop circles", mandalas that appear in fields. The mandala forms are created when some of the plants in the field bend while the others stay erect. The lines are very distinct and look as if they were made by a machine. The bent-over plants are not damaged and continue growing. Occasionally crop circles are simple, and sometimes they appear as very complex geometric structures. Farmers from all over the world have reported crop circles in their fields for many generations. In recent years these crop circles have been photographed and documented from airplanes. Researchers are trying to understand the cause of this phenomenon. The reasons for their appearance remain controversial. Scientists and academics think they are man-made, but there are those who think that aliens from outer space are trying to communicate using mandala forms.

An Expression of Belief in God

The symbol of the circle has been used by religions throughout the world in various ceremonies to express yearning for divine perfection.

In Judaism, the Star of David is based on the division of the circle into six parts and expresses the balance between the masculine and the feminine. The Tree of Life in the Kabbalah, also based on a mandalic form, expresses a view of the world and humanity's place in the universe in relation to the Divine. In the Tree of Life, ten circles (sephirot) are drawn, symbolizing the divine abundance that is directed toward humanity as a beam of light. The ten sephirot are screens, or filters, through which the light passes to adjust it to the human dimension. The Zohar (a group of books at the heart of Jewish mysticism) relates to the bindu point as the centre of creation of everything in the world.

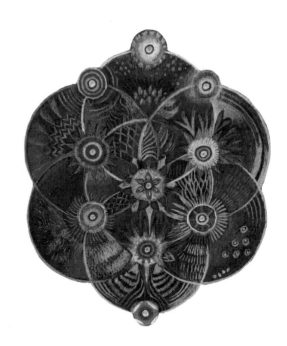

The Tree of Life, according to the Kabbalah, displays the ten sephirot between God and man.

"There is no circle in the world that comes not from the one point in the centre ... and this point which stands in the centre takes all the light and illuminates the body, and everything is illuminated."

(Tishbi, volume 1: Remez).

In Eastern religions, mandalas are built on the principle that our body is a temple and that divinity dwells within, in the centre. The mandala is used as a tool for religious ritual, training and study related to purifying the soul and releasing it from the earthly chains that are an obstacle to a life of happiness. The Hindu mandala is called yantra, meaning a tool for liberation, and refers to the mandala's wonderful ability to release the soul from its bonds of illusion and suffering and transport it to the glorious realm of absolute happiness.

Enso is Japanese for "circle". The calligraphic sign of the circle drawn with a special brush symbolizes enlightenment, strength, elegance, the world and empty space. The enso is an expression of the fleeting moment. According to Japanese Zen Buddhism, drawing the enso expresses the painter's spiritual development at that moment. Many students of Zen draw the enso as a daily meditation practice. Sometimes the circle is closed and sometimes it remains open. The open part of the enso symbolizes that the circle doesn't stand on its own, but is part of larger circles. This imperfection is an essential part of human existence. Many Zen teachers adopt the enso as their personal signature.

In Christianity, the mandala appears in the large, impressive, coloured stained-glass windows of Gothic cathedrals. These windows are called rosettas because of their similarity to the rose flower. They were created so that divine light would shine on the believers through the perfect circle, inducing a sacred atmosphere.

The prohibition against drawing animals and human figures in Islam encouraged artists to use geometrical shapes constructed from symmetrical circular structures. We can see the decorative designs on the ceramic tiles on the walls of mosques and luxurious palaces of the sultans. Muslim believers write the many names of Allah in circles using colourful stylized calligraphy.

Carl Jung and the Mandala

The Swiss psychiatrist Carl Jung is undoubtedly the person most responsible for bringing the ancient knowledge of mandala drawing to the attention of the Western world. Through his keen curiosity and personal investigation, he discovered the power of the mandala as a tool for self-expression and emotional and psychic work. Using himself as the subject of his research, he developed a method that uses mandala drawings as a therapeutic tool.

In 1913 Jung was 38 years old with an established, successful career as a psychiatrist. However, following a falling out with his revered teacher, Sigmund Freud, he experienced irresolvable conflicts within his soul. His behaviour became strange; he grew distant from friends and left his teaching position. He withdrew to his home on Lake Zurich, built miniature villages and collected rocks on which he inscribed esoteric phrases in Latin. In his search for inner communication, he even began dreaming of an encounter with Elijah the Prophet. After three years, toward the end of his crisis, he began to draw mandalas.

"I drew the first mandala in 1916," he wrote in his memoirs, "and apparently I still didn't understand what it meant then. Every morning during the war in 1918, I'd doodle little circles, mandalas, in my notebook to suit my mood that day. I was able to see the daily changes that were going on in my soul from these drawings."

Jung continued drawing mandalas for ten years. Drawing circles helped him heal the broken fragments of his soul. Based on his personal experience, he consolidated a theory of the mandala's essence. According to Jung, the mandala represents the entire psyche, the conscious and unconscious together; creating a mandala awakens the source of the soul and a sense of complete satisfaction. He identified with the spiritual adventures of the alchemists in Europe – very far from the scientific spirit of his time. The ancient science of alchemy was common in 12th- and 13th-century Europe. The alchemists believed that by combining certain elements they would discover hidden magical powers – the "philosopher's stone" – that would transform cheap metals into gold and silver, as well as a cure for diseases that would give them eternal life.

In 1930, after delving deeply into Chinese philosophy, Jung gave a seminar on the mandala in Berlin. At the conference he presented mandalas drawn by his patients alongside Tibetan mandalas, Navajo sand paintings and alchemic writings from the Middle Ages. He described images in dreams of patients never exposed to alchemy that contained mandalas and alchemic symbols such as a snake swallowing its tail, a blue flower and a red ball. Jung called these images "archetypes". Archetypes are universal symbols passed from generation to generation in all cultures in what Jung termed "the collective unconscious".

According to Jung, the circle's centre is the source of energy – the seat of the feeling of self. Opposites unite at this point. Jung differentiates between traditional mandalas drawn according to a defined, objective format and mandalas drawn freely and spontaneously, an expression of the individual and the changing state of the soul. He believed that mandalas are created in dreams or times of wakefulness when the unconscious is called to heal itself. Jung considered that each person's unique individuation process was very important, giving a person a life of meaning, a sense of worth, power and energy to think and create.

In his memoirs, Jung wrote, "When I began to draw mandalas, I saw that everything, all the paths I had been following, all the steps I had taken, were leading back to a single point – namely, to the mid-point. It became increasingly plain to me that the mandala is the centre. It is the exponent of all paths. It is the path to the centre, to individuation."

Jung emphasizes that "... creating mandalas has a healing influence on the doer only when it is done spontaneously and not as an artificial or direct imitation of similar images.

"The mandala is not something that one decides about, rather it is something that must grow from the dark depths of oblivion; only then will it be a transcendental expression of earlier senses of consciousness and intuition of the spirit".

Jung describes how his patients painted very complex mandalas without having the slightest idea of their meaning. In this case, mandala painting is a new direction for the soul, as yet unconscious, a reorganization of the complete personality. The strict form of the mandala compensates for the confusion and lack of order because of the central point to which everything relates. The centre also serves as an anchor point for opposites.

A mandala must contain some kind of opening, something that breaks the symmetry and balance and from which a process comes that will lead to the dismantling of the old mandala and the creation of the next mandala. The existence of this process is also dependent on the ability to let go of the existing mandala and let it die. It is not right to hold onto the mandala that yesterday reflected balance. What was yesterday a symbol of life might turn into a symbol of death and degeneration of a process of searching for the self which has reached a standstill. Therefore it is not worthwhile to cling to and identify with it; better to let it go and let it disband. From the dismantling of the mandala, a new world is born, and the individual is reborn again into the world. The endeavour to reach wholeness within the self will collide again and again with reality, and each time this conflict will cause the dismantling of the mandala so that it can be born anew. What remains from the experience of creating the mandala is the memory of a glimpse of the eternal through a window inside us that has opened. There is no choice but to face the fact that life consists of continual, dynamic change, uncertainty and insecurity, which is even more true of the creative process.

The process of creating a work of art parallels the process of spontaneously creating a mandala that expresses a new unity. Creating the work of art should provide a feeling of reconciliation, harmony and balance of inner tensions. However, an authentic creator never reaches their goal; they are always in the process. The completion of one work may give birth to the seedling from which a new creation will grow.

The mandala symbolizes both the end and the beginning, as well as the cyclical nature of the beginning and the end that returns again and again throughout a person's life. When the unity that a person tries to preserve through small adaptive changes gives birth to new unities, then the old mandala that provides sanctuary within its protective circles may become a place of birth. "Mandalas are places of birth in the literal sense of the word, the lotus flowers within which the Buddha awakens to life," said Jung. Within them something new may be born, and from them one can go forth to a new life.

Jung's First Mandala

Jung drew his first mandala in 1916 and called it "The System of all the Worlds". You can find what it looks like with a quick search online. According to Jung, the circle represents the world, and it is divided into four parts. The upper part belongs to the gods and the light of wisdom, while the lower part is our dualistic physical world. To the right is the pure, feminine and spiritual, and on the left, the masculine, sexual and dark.

The mandala represents both the macro-cosmos and the micro-cosmos. The circles within the mandala are replicated and duplicated alternately inside and outside. What is outside is inside and what is inside mirrors the outside. In Jung's mandala we can identify various mythological symbols he called "archetypes".

At the top is the mythological god Panas who was born from a winged egg. Panas is one of the first deities ever formed and represents the light of the sun and wisdom; later his name was changed to Eros, the god of love. The seven-branched candelabra below him flickers in the light of spirituality. To the lamp's right is a winged serpent symbolizing art, and to the lamp's left is a winged mouse representing science.

The lower section holds the Egyptian god Abraxas, with a serpent's body and lion's head adorned with ten rays of yellow light. Abraxas represents duality: good and bad, light and shadow, conscious and unconscious. The name Abraxas in numerology is 365, the number of days in the year. The tree of life springs forth from him. To Abraxas' left is the monster of death and to his right is the animal representing death and rebirth.

On the mandala's feminine right side, a sacred dove (representing the Holy Spirit) spreads its wings. It bursts forth from a two-tiered chalice representing divine wisdom and the light of the Garden of Eden. To the right of the chalice there is a purple ball and two additional planets.

On the mandala's masculine left side, a snake appears, winding around two male sexual organs, one red and the other blue, together representing the body's circulatory system. Next to them we can identify the darkness of outer space as a huge ball and the moon in two states, one completely darkened and the other partially lit.

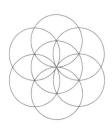

CHAPTER 3
DRAWING MANDALAS

Unlike other art activities, sketching a mandala does not require prior artistic knowledge or skills. It is an intuitive form of sketching that anyone can do. Everyone has creative ability just waiting to express itself in the world. Life itself is a never-ending, moment-to-moment creation. Through the mandala we let the life force manifest. We drew uninhibitedly as children, but the comments we heard regarding how "talented" we were often put an end to our enjoyment of expressing ourselves through colour and creativity. Mandala sketching is an opportunity to return to and use the natural creative force present in each of us. To truly discover the power of the mandala, it is important to disengage from all outside criticism and focus solely on your inner world.

In the process of creating a mandala, it is impossible to make a mistake. It doesn't matter what you sketch. What is important is the sense of presence during the process. The best way to sketch a mandala is to just dive in without prior thinking or planning. We must feel confident that our unique creation is just right for us and always leads us toward self-healing and wholeness. We are always in a process of growing, changing and developing. By allowing ourselves to be wholeheartedly present in the process, lowering expectations and suspending judgement, we can create with the joy of a child. By doing this we connect to our inner truth and let it flow outward in a natural way. A wonderful artist hides within each person, desiring to express their unique, personal perspective of reality.

Through creating the mandala, we come closer to the meaning of our lives and the purpose we were born to. We let our soul tell its stories, express the unknown and introduce pictures from our imaginations. The mandala creates a "safe space" for expressing unknown parts of our personality, thereby releasing them into the visible world. By transferring them to the conscious realm, we can take personal responsibility for our spiritual and mental development and connect all our parts into a whole being.

The Supplies You Will Need

- Compass that can be "locked" in place (so that the same radius can easily be used again)
- Ruler, preferably transparent
- HB, B3 and B6 drawing pencils (in the US these are #1 and #2 pencils)
- Eraser, pencil sharpener, scissors and glue
- Round paint brushes, numbers 3 and 5
- Pallette for mixing colours
- Block of white 240g drawing paper
- Set of assorted coloured felt tip markers (at least 24 different shades)
- A large variety of coloured pencils, watercolours, gouache paint

The first stage in creating a mandala is to sketch the template or pattern. There are countless templates on which to base your mandala. As a way of introduction into the rich world of mandalas, I have chosen 16 templates that constitute stages in the development of the mandala. I recommend sketching the mandala templates in the order they are presented. After gaining experience through the mandala way, you can choose templates according to your own interests and preferences. In each of the 16 lessons, we first learn to sketch the template and then, after a brief meditation, we go on to create the mandala.

We always begin work on the mandala in the centre, at the bindu point. This centre point connects us to creative energy, provides a focus, gives us strength, balance and self-confidence and enables us to surrender to the here and now. From the bindu point, we will sketch from the energy that exists at hidden levels of the unconscious.

We work on the mandala from a place of internal freedom and flow. At the end of the time allocated, or when we have finished, we move on to the stages of observation, contemplation and documentation of the process we experienced.

Finally, we try to decipher and understand the messages we received from the mandala; we can examine and interpret the mandala by ourselves or within a group.

Stage One: Sketching the Template

The template is made from combinations of various geometric shapes. Each template represents a different perspective of reality. A square within a circle, for example, represents a view of life within the limitations of matter. The square represents the limits of the material while the circle represents liberation, freedom and infinity.

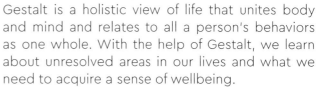

The use of templates in *The Mandala Way* is based on Gestalt theory, which sees the world in patterns. Gestalt is a holistic view of life that unites body and mind and relates to all a person's behaviors as one whole. With the help of Gestalt, we learn about unresolved areas in our lives and what we need to acquire a sense of wellbeing.

Each chapter priovdes detailed instructions on how to sketch the template. Try it first on scratch paper and then on good-quality paper or canvas.

Stage Two: Meditation

The time we spend sketching the mandala is quality time with ourselves. The meditation helps us to focus on our inner world and quiet outside noises. Each mandala template has its own meditation which directs us to that template's unique qualities. It is desirable, though not necessary, to meditate after sketching the template, rather than before. This gives us the opportunity to ponder the meaning of the mandala more deeply.

How to Meditate?

First, you must set aside a time when you can take a break from your regular schedule. Find a pleasant, quiet, ventilated space where you feel comfortable. You may want to light a candle or incense and/or turn on soft music that you like in the background.

Sit in a comfortable position on a chair or pillow. Make sure that your spine is erect but relaxed. Imagine a ring connected to a taut string attached to the crown of your head pulling your spine upwards, creating space and letting your lungs open wide. Close your eyes and focus on your breathing. Air enters, air exits. With each out breath, imagine that you are releasing all the tension stored in your body. Take seven deep breaths. If thoughts enter your mind, simply take note and gently release them to continue on their way. Concentrate on the air that enters and exits your body. Tightly tense the muscles of your eyes, lips, shoulders, arms, hands, buttocks, stomach, legs and feet. Then relax each body part, one after the other. Repeat this tensing and relaxing.

Meditate using the appropriate meditation for the template you are about to make.

Then slowly open your eyes, return to the here and now and begin to work on the mandala.

Stage Three: Working on the Mandala

There are only two rules in creating a mandala:

- Begin in the centre, from the bindu point.
- There are no rules!

Look at the various colours before you. Which colour catches your eye? Without thinking, take this colour and use it to colour the central point. This is the bindu: the starting point, the spark that gives life to the creation. The mandala sketching expands from the centre outwards, with no mental effort.

Continue working on the first circle around the centre point, bearing in mind what you just drew. Each additional circle relates in form or colour to the previous circle, thus creating an internal dialogue between the circles.

It is important to work with your intuition and enter the rhythm of sketching in circles. A circular movement, like ripples in water, creates a circle within a circle. The degree of freedom as you work on the mandala is very significant. We can see its expression in whether we work within the template lines or whether we decide to ignore the template altogether.

Remember, there is no right or wrong. Everything is an intuitive choice – of colours, lines, surface areas and techniques. Send your critical nature on vacation. Let the movement of your hand flow over the paper freely as you become increasingly attentive to yourself and your inner knowing.

While you work, ask yourself questions: What do you want? What suits you? What colour is right for you to use at any particular moment? Try to stay connected to the centre point of the mandala throughout. You may want to go back to add or change earlier circles, which is fine.

Working in stages recreates life's cycles: the days of the week, changing seasons, passing years. The mandala, like the circles of life, can continue to grow without end.

Decide on a period of time that suits you – once a week, once every two weeks or once a month – and sketch more mandalas using the same template. Notice if there is some kind of development or an interesting sequence among the sketches.

When Do You Stop?

Either you run out of paper or you run out of time. It is recommended to allocate at least one hour to each session. When the time is up, it can be called "stopping" rather than "finishing". You can return and continue to work on the mandala, after even a few days or a week. Different mandalas can require different amounts and rhythms of time to complete.

The best time to stop is after completing a circle in the mandala and not in the middle of working on a circle. It is easier to continue if the previous process (i.e. circle) is completed... just like in life.

You may sketch in open or closed spaces. You can sketch symbols or figures. Give your hand free rein and think as little as possible. Allow things to come up from the unconscious.

Try not to be critical. Everything that happens is correct, exact and expresses the inner self. Remember, criticism blocks. It is important to work on the mandala effortlessly, with no pressure or task orientation. In this way we experience our inner desires.

When you complete the mandala, hang it where you can look at it for a while. Mandalas radiate energy of healing and blessing. You can sketch mandalas in a small group setting. This allows you to share your experience and listen to the experience of others.

Stage Four: Observing the Process

Interpreting the mandala begins with observing the process that we went through while creating it.

Observation helps us to understand a bit more about ourselves: Where were we emotionally, mentally, energetically and physically while we were sketching the mandala? A great deal of knowledge is hidden in our unconscious. Mandala sketching allows us to sketch out this knowledge and transfer it to consciousness, so that we can identify the issues that we are struggling with. It is recommended to have a notebook available to record your observations of the process.

We can document the process of creating a mandala in graphic map form, similar to the thought maps used by Leonardo da Vinci when he wanted to chronicle his ideas. Making a map is particularly suited to intuitive, naturally flowing thoughts as opposed to linear, logical thoughts. The map helps us see how each detail of our experience relates to and then gives birth to a fresh detail.

Place a small circle to represent the mandala you created in the centre of a piece of white paper. Sketch four diagonal lines branching out from it in different directions. Each line focuses on a different aspect of the experience.

The energy component

is represented by the element of fire. Here we write about our energy and enthusiasm during the drawing process. Did I work passionately or with a sense of boredom? Did I relate to the drawing like a task that must be completed or with inner freedom? Did the mandala take form effortlessly or did I feel stuck?

At the end I didn't want to stop drawing

What am I doing here?

Shoulders are connected to burdens

The physical component

is represented by the element of earth. Here we write about physical sensations that we felt while drawing. Did I experience a change of heartbeat or breathing, sweating, muscle contractions, feelings of hot or cold, thirst or hunger?

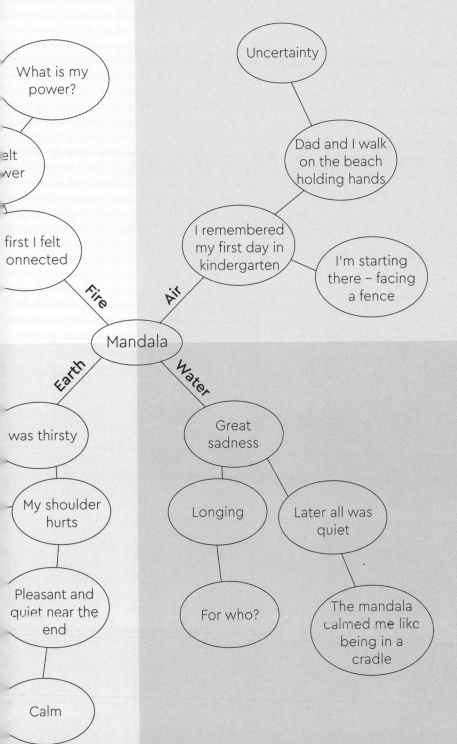

The mental component

is represented by the element of air. Here we write our thoughts, visions and the memories that came to us while drawing. Did distant childhood memories arise? Did I remember someone significant in my life? Did I think of a creative idea or did I come up with a solution to a problem that has been worrying me?

The emotional component

is represented by the element of water. Here we write the emotions we felt during the drawing process: anger, fear, happiness, love, etc. Did I feel that I was in an emotional whirlpool or in a stable, orderly place? As I drew, did I feel that I was in a free and open space or in a closed and suffocating space? Did the drawing bring up emotional pain or a pleasant feeling?

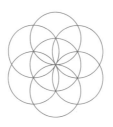

CHAPTER 4
INTERPRETING MANDALAS

There are many ways to interpret a mandala. The most important thing is to take a nonjudgemental approach and remember there are no good or bad elements. All the shapes, colours and figures tell a story. I call this "seeing a movie", with every artist as the director. The messages arrive of their own accord as you contemplate the mandala. Sometimes they come as clear words, as "movies" or images, all of which become the basis for deeper understanding. The mandala shines a spotlight on the place where we are standing and lights the path ahead.

At the beginning of my journey, I wasn't sure how to teach the art of interpreting a mandala, but through years of experience I have formulated a practical method to "read" mandalas.

It is important to note that there is not just one way to "read" a mandala. We can raise questions based on elements in the mandala either consciously or unconsciously. These questions can then lead to a conversation or an inner dialogue that broaden the creator's perspective.

We first look at the mandala in general without focusing on any details. What kind of energy does it transmit? For example, does the energy burst forth or converge inwardly? Is it diffused or focused?

Next we scrutinize the details that comprise the mandala. It is important to let go of criticism and judgement. Allow it to awaken an inner dialogue and see it as a positive force that can help, advance and empower us.

Even if we feel confused or unsure, this can be a starting point for change. We are always in search of growth, flow and balance. When interpreting someone else's mandala, we must be careful and kind, viewing things from the perspective of the mandala's creator. Remarks do not provide definitive answers, but rather raise questions and prompt discussion. Emphasize the positive and remember that deep listening has healing qualities.

The stages of observation and interpretation are described in this chapter in order of importance. Be sure not to jump to conclusions at any stage. The final understanding comes at the end of the process. We first look at how we related to the template itself and then we examine the elements within the template. These include the poles, colours and four elements, the images and shapes.

Opposite is an example of how to interpret a mandala using all seven stages of observation and interpretation we are about to discuss.

2. Elements within the Template

Strong focus on the bindu and the first circle. "Me against the world, with no close or family support circles".

1. Template

Did not stick to the template form. Focus on the central circle, but have the courage to choose where your mandala will go and what form it will take. Don't give in to external influences, but instead work from within.

3. Two Poles

Circular movement with no regard for the poles, suggesting a feeling of loneliness, with no anchors to hold onto.

4. Colour

Strong, intense primary colours. The blue creates a separation. The yellow gives a feeling of warmth and burning.

7. Images

The many eyes in the outer circle surround the inner circle. They suggest a feeling of critical observation of the world.

6. Shapes

Thick, broken lines in the centre of the mandala, like cracked earth. The quick, restless lines outside suggest the energy of fire.

5. Four Elements

Combination of fire and earth energies. The fire is trapped inside and tries to shake up the earthly framework, like overflowing lava in a volcano.

1. Template

The template is a given form. Our brain chooses to see the template in a subjective manner. An example of this is our relation to our body. All people are born into the template of a body with limitations, but we can relate to this template in different ways. We can resist and oppose our body by neglect, or we can take care of it by nurturing and nourishing it.

The mandalas are based on different templates. Each template pattern relates to a different aspect of our worldview. The Flower of Life template, for example, is built on infinite multiplication, reflecting freedom of choice. Drawing this mandala connects us to our feelings about boundaries and limitations versus personal freedom. If we work in a group, we will discover that each person sees something different in the Flower of Life template. How each person sees the mandala is an indication of that person's soul and how they experience the world. This expression can then be extrapolated to other aspects of his life. For example, if the drawer of the mandala emphasized the borders or felt imprisoned by them, we might hypothesize that in real life, they are struggling with an internal or external authority, which is imposing restrictions. If the painter emphasized areas within the template, we can suppose that their conflict is related more to whatever is in the framework. Ignoring the template altogether can indicate that a person is focusing on what they want and less on what is expected of them or, on the contrary, it can be a kind of rebellion that ignores external demands and challenges.

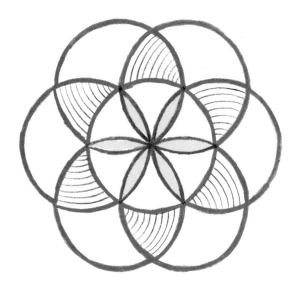

The emphasis on the contours suggests the need to adhere to and emphasize frameworks and laws.

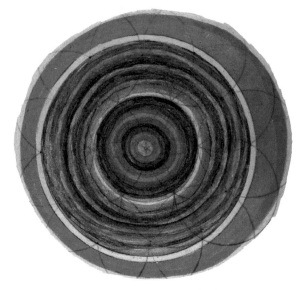

The painter ignored the Seed of Life template. Ignoring the template suggests an inner process and the courage to choose a different, independent path.

2. Elements within the Template

The circle and the mandala template represent our worldview, which is constantly expanding from the centre outwards. The bindu and the first circle, or that area closest to the circle's centre, tell about our relationship to ourselves and our internal world. Notice the different shapes in the area of the first circle: was it quiet and pleasant to be there? Or were you impatient to reach the outer areas of the mandala? The guiding principle for interpreting the elements of the template is that the closer we are to the bindu, the closer we are to the centre of the self and, conversely, the further away from the bindu, the more we are in touch with the outside world, which is expressed primarily in our personal relationships. The mandala's background symbolizes the rest of the world for us. There are instances where we can see a direct, strong and energetic connection with the world, and there are times when the inner world is closed off.

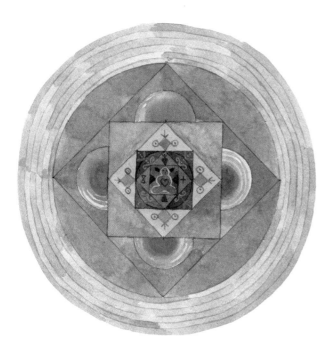

The image withdraws into an inner world. There is a feeling of warmth and acceptance in the adjoining environment. At the same time, there is a feeling of distance from what is going on outside.

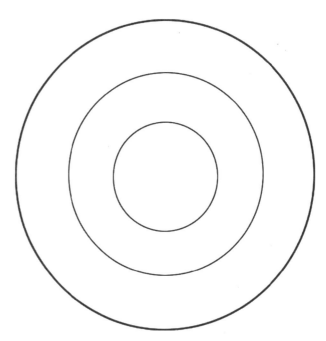

My relationship to myself.
My relationship to my immediate environment.
My relationship to the more distant environment.
My relationship to the world.

3. Two Poles

Humanity's view of the world is dualistic. We live below, on the earth's surface, and the sky is above us. Our bodies are divided into two sides: right and left. The feeling of being connected to the poles provides a sense of stability and security. When we look at the mandala, our unique worldview is reflected. According to Jung, the world within the mandala is divided into the conscious world, in the upper half of the circle, and the unconscious world, in the lower half. The right half is the active, doing, masculine part, whereas the left half is the feminine, feeling, dreaming and intuitive part. When we contemplate the mandala, we can discern what we drew in the different parts of the circle and gain understanding about our feelings in relation to the subject of each part.

The polarities in our body first come into being when the sperm and the egg meet: our bindu point, from where we begin our journey on earth. The egg is filled with negatively charged energy and the sperm is filled with positively charged energy, just like an electric battery. The positive energy is one of imparting and giving; the negative energy receives and contains.

Our bodies have two poles. The north pole is in the chest and the south pole resides in the lower abdomen. The two horizontal poles are connected by a middle line that connects the energies of the earth's surface and the cosmos above. This connection enables us to live with a sense of power, fullness and satisfaction. The power of the poles differs from person to person and is influenced by external factors like weather conditions, geographic location, seasonal changes, the food we eat and the relationships we form.

We can divide the mandala circle into four parts:

- Above – the visible world, the world of light and sky, the relationship with the father, thoughts, desires, aspirations and goals.
- Below – the world of night, the unconscious, the relationship to mother earth, sensuality, containment, nurturance, safety.
- Right – the active, masculine force that acts and creates in the world.
- Left – the passive, feminine force that is sensitive, contains and receives.

Opposite is an example of how to interpret a mandala by dividing it into four parts.

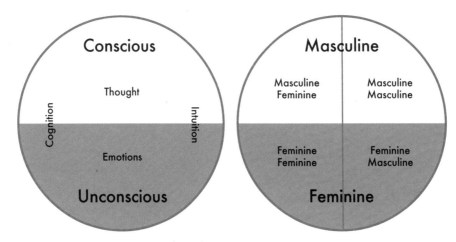

The treetop and fruit growing toward the light symbolize results and achievements.

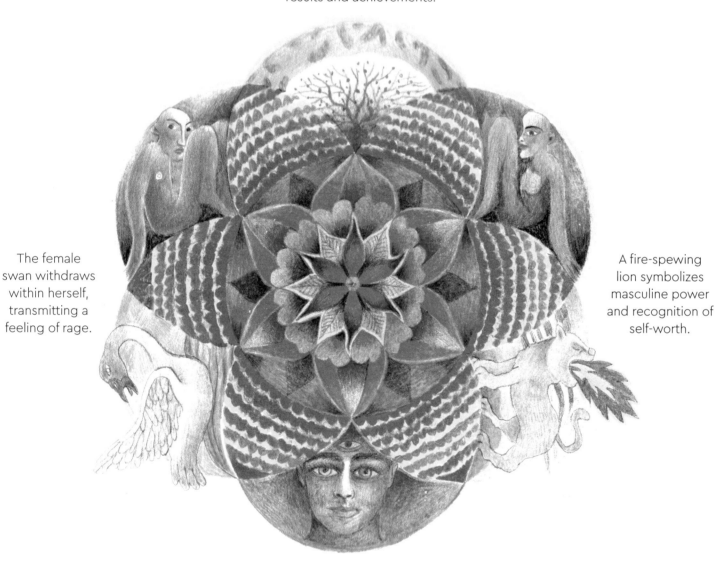

The female swan withdraws within herself, transmitting a feeling of rage.

A fire-spewing lion symbolizes masculine power and recognition of self-worth.

The third eye symbolizes our ability to see beyond the five senses and receive messages from the unconscious.

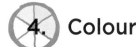

4. Colour

Colours – whether of clothing, furniture, the walls, foods, flowers and even the sky – influence us in various ways. Each colour and shade has a frequency that sends us energy. Colours arouse emotions and memories. Some people are strongly drawn to specific colours that others are deterred by. Orange stimulates the appetite, while red energizes doing. Companies use colour in their logos to increase the selling power of their products; for example, Coca-Cola uses energetic bright red to enhance the image that Coke is "the taste of life". In times of mourning and bereavement, we wear black, and at weddings the bride wears pure white as a symbol of virgin innocence.

Everything we see is made visible by direct or reflected light rays, made of waves. Colour is determined according to the length of the wave. Human vision is limited to the length of light waves in what is called the "visible range". Light visible to humans is only a minute part of the huge scale of wavelengths found in nature. The longest visible light wave is red; the shortest wave is violet. All the colours we see lie in between red and violet on the scale. White light is a mixture of all the wavelengths and black is perceived as a colour that swallows or absorbs the light rays.

All the colours in the world are composed of three primary colours: red, yellow and blue. Red symbolizes the building of tissues and the mental and physical digestive system. It points to building, growth and the struggle for life. Red is associated with the warm, pulsing blood within us. Yellow is the colour representing the great guardian of the soul. The yellow of the sun represents the elements that act and create in the external world, as well as the more rational and logical parts. Yellow is the ego we identify with, our unique personality, and symbolizes what we know about our story. Blue is the colour of the unexamined depths of the soul. The dark blue of the ocean depths where the powers of dissolution and destruction lie, for example, is like the power to digest food and nourish cells with new life energy. Blue represents death and rebirth. These three primary colours represent the three forces continually active in our body and soul to varying degrees. Red is the force that builds; yellow is the force that maintains, acts and responds; and blue is the dismantling force that enables new building.

Intermediate shades and combinations of primary colours create infinite tones in the universe. Each tone or shade has its own unique significance. Dark or light colours also reflect our mental state. For example, if we prefer very stimulating colours with a strong presence, we reflect a worldview that identifies with strong energy and dynamic conflict. Pale, weak colours indicate passivity and dislike of conflict, a tendency to preserve the status quo and avoid making waves. If we tend to add shades of grey to light colours, this can be an indication of melancholy and depression.

Throughout history, in all cultures, humans have given a variety of meanings to colours. Some colours represent human characteristics. For example, in Western culture, white symbolizes purity. According to astrological classifications, each planet has a different colour as an attribute. Red, for example, is associated with Mars, and the sign of Aries.

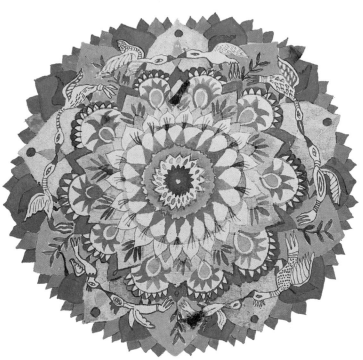

Spring
Strong colours create surprising encounters between one colour and another, and give a feeling of blossoming and growth.

Summer
Shades of yellow, a warm, powerful colour, overflowing, without borders and full of movement.

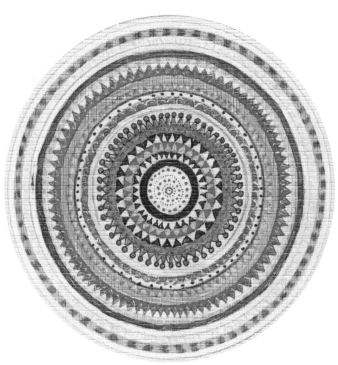

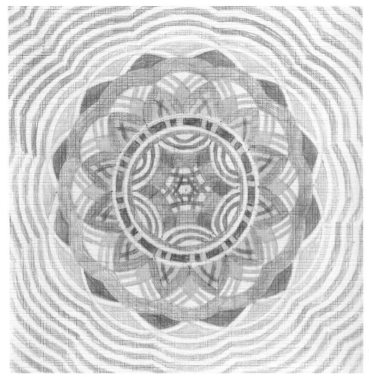

Autumn
Gentle colours tending toward cool shades bring a feeling of melancholy, closing up and internal listening.

Winter
Gloomy colours and grey tones suggest a static, introverted feeling.

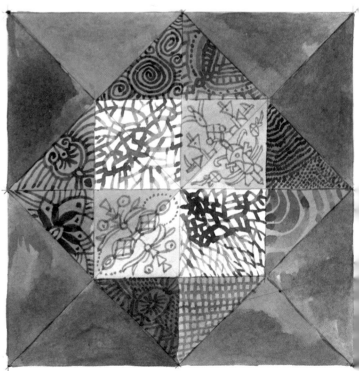

Interpreting the Feelings That Colours Arouse in You

The colours may represent different things for different people. Take some time to consider what thoughts, emotions and sensations each colour arouses in you. They may be similar to those below, or they may be unique to you.

Red: life energy, stimulating, frenetic

Orange: intimacy, excitement, enthusiasm

Yellow: focus, intellect, action, freedom

Green: development, growth, harmony

Blue: tranquility, calm, safety, trust, efficiency

Purple: spiritual, unconscious, intuition, melancholy

White: purity, neutrality

Black: absorption, reduction, darkness, despondency

Grey: restraint, moderation, boredom

Brown: stability, reliability, ground, stuck

Pink: love, joy, sensitivity

Silver: feminine power, sensitivity, passivity

Gold: masculine power, royalty

Turquoise: release, friendship, freedom, ease

Light blue: distance, clarity, balance

Maroon: strength, commitment, impulses

5. Four Elements

The ancient Greeks were the first to conceive of the idea that the natural world was based on a small number of material elements, like the chemical elements of modern times. This idea was most successfully espoused by the philosopher Empedocles, of the Pythagorean School, who claimed that all materials were compounds of four elements: earth, water, air and fire. Later a 'fifth element, ether, was added. Ether was the source of the celestial bodies. With time, the elements were given deeper meanings and became part of various philosophical and mystical theories.

Each element has distinctive characteristics according to the spiritual, mental and physical attributes it represents. As we look at the general energy that our mandala transmits, its unique colours and shapes, we can identify the various elements.

Fire

Energy, erupting, action-inducing, passion, willpower, clarity, creativity, initiative, intuition

The element of fire is an expression of energy and creation. To deeply understand it, envision standing by a roaring bonfire, looking at the flames leaping and changing every second. The strong energetic movement of the fire's dance is like the dance of life, changing and recreating itself each moment. You can't contain fire; you can't hold it down. Fire will immediately die in a closed container; it needs air to continue burning. The fire

element needs freedom and space to burn and give light and warmth. Fire appears in an infinite variety of changing shapes and colours. When fire is burning under control, it warms and nourishes, but when it burns out of control it can consume all that is in its path.

Fire has the power to melt metal and change its state from solid to liquid. The sun, the ball of fire that we revolve around, is the source of light and heat that makes life on earth possible. Fire and the sun symbolize the masculine side, the creator, initiator, acting overtly and consciously. People whose dominant element is fire are day people, full of enthusiasm, unafraid, honest, impulsive, charismatic, initiators, changing and lacking patience for slower people. Generally they are leaders with great personal charm. The animal representing the fire element is the lion, king of the animals.

Water

Liquid, emotion, internal experience, feminine, passive motion, containing

Tempestuous seas, a seasonal stream, a quiet lake, fish in a pool, pouring rain, streaming tears – these are all images associated with the element of water. Water is an expression of the realm of emotions. Emotions can sometimes be stormy with anger and sadness, and sometimes happy, quiet and tranquil like water in a pool. Water is moved by external factors; it lacks fire's internal source of creation. Water is moved by the wind and according to nature's laws of gravitational pull on the changing surface of the earth.

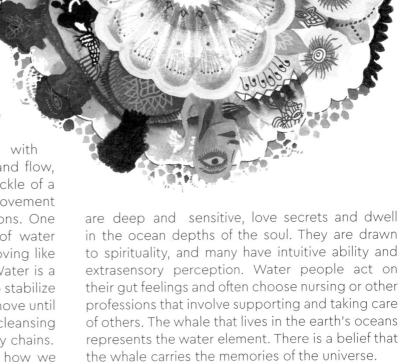

The water element is associated with feminine energy. The ocean tide's ebb and flow, the fullness of a rushing river and the trickle of a seasonal stream symbolize the cyclical movement of the female, like the full and new moons. One can imagine the changing conditions of water like the alternating states of the soul, moving like a pendulum between joy and sadness. Water is a passive element that needs a container to stabilize and confine it within a shape. Water will move until it reaches balance. Water symbolizes the cleansing and purification of the soul from its earthly chains.

The element of water is the basis of how we experience the world, of our ability to enjoy colours, smells and tastes, and get to know and understand others. People whose dominant element is water are deep and sensitive, love secrets and dwell in the ocean depths of the soul. They are drawn to spirituality, and many have intuitive ability and extrasensory perception. Water people act on their gut feelings and often choose nursing or other professions that involve supporting and taking care of others. The whale that lives in the earth's oceans represents the water element. There is a belief that the whale carries the memories of the universe.

Air

Gas, principle of motion, flow, freedom, understanding, wisdom, logic

The air element symbolizes thought and clear perceptions. Air contains "prana", or life energy. In addition to the oxygen we breathe, we also absorb through our breathing a spark of cosmic life. The animal symbolizing the air element is the eagle, particularly the white eagle. Just as the eagle, king of birds, flies high in the sky, among the clouds, looking at and examining the world below from above, so, too, air people look at the world with a general and philosophical perspective. They would rather observe and study social phenomena than have hands-on experience of it. Air people are artists, philosophers, scientists and thinkers. The air element symbolizes pure, abstract thought like the transparent air that can't be seen. Air is the highest and most spiritual dimension and does not interfere, like God who looks down on the universe. The element of air is essentially masculine, in need of freedom and wide spaces, and spreads out in all directions. It is the element that affects the other three elements: it fans the fire, stirs up the waters and blows across the earth, turning it to sand and dust. Air people act logically and need room to maneuver. They are thought to be congenial and avoid direct conflict; their language is spiced with humour, ease and cynicism. Air represents openness, innovation, communication and the love of conversation and debate. Air people choose communications, teaching and science for professions and always feel they know the real truth.

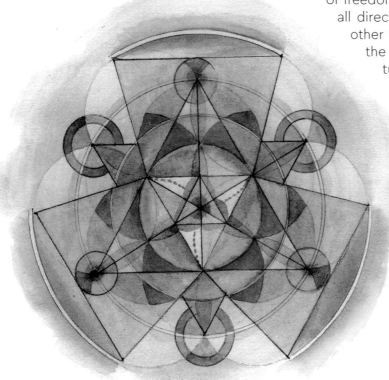

Earth

Solid, base, sensory perception, tradition, feeling of belonging, pleasure, gathering

The earth element is the element of our material roots. From dust we come and to dust we shall return. To stand firmly on the earth with both feet on the ground symbolizes a hold on reality and a feeling of confidence that the earth brings to our lives. We can envision the slow walk of the bull, the animal that represents the earth element, as it patiently and purposefully creates straight furrows in the ground.

The earth represents the inevitable need for rules and laws. Cyclical frameworks and ceremonies provide a sense of stability and security. Earth is a feminine element, symbolizing the great mother that gives and takes life. Mother Earth nourishes and nurtures her children, provides a framework and educates them how to act in the world through clear, strict rules. Earth people are the conservatives among us, the ambitious achievers that obstinately stick to their objectives. They are practical, patient and stubborn, enabling them to reach excellence in whatever they do. Most earth people are economically comfortable since material abundance is important to them. They are generally slow to take care of their bodies and enjoy good food and excellent, elegantly served wine. Through this element we connect to all the solid chemical elements, precious stones, crystals with healing properties and various metals like silver and gold. The earth element is symbolized by the physical body, the chariot of the soul. We are nourished by the fruits of the earth and connected to vegetation, flowers and animals. Through the earth element we connect to our five senses and are in touch with reality.

6. Shapes

Our hand movements as we draw express feelings and emotions which can be interpreted just like a graphologist interprets handwriting. Interpreting the shapes in a drawing is parallel to reading a person's body language. Feelings of power and strength are expressed by energetic movements represented, for example, by heavy lines or filled-in areas.

To map the infinite possibilities of expressing basic elements in shapes, I have divided familiar shapes schematically into four categories in the table opposite: dots, lines, shapes and surface areas.

The dot is a primary element and can include all the small forms. A group of dots creates different kinds of lines: straight and curving, broken and jagged. Lines in different combinations create different effects within the closed shapes. There are, of course, an infinite number of shapes. In this category we can differentiate between shapes formed from straight lines, representing the left, logical side of the brain, and more amorphous shapes, representing the right, intuitive side of the brain. The surface area refers to the space within the shapes. There are infinite possibilities for filling these areas; for example, using strong or pale colours, different textures or designs such as dots.

The Different Shapes in a Mandala

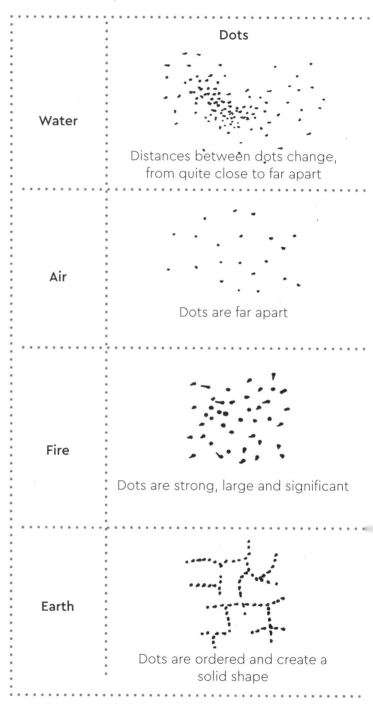

	Dots
Water	Distances between dots change, from quite close to far apart
Air	Dots are far apart
Fire	Dots are strong, large and significant
Earth	Dots are ordered and create a solid shape

Lines	Shapes	Surface area

 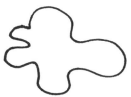 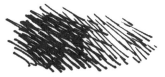

| Softly curving flow | Imprecise, amorphic forms | Varying textures with unclear borders |

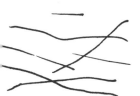 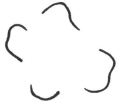 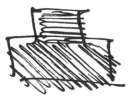

| Mostly sharp, thin ...ating straight lines | Open forms left to the imagination to complete | Precise, uniform filling |

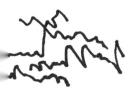 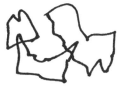 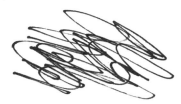

| ...harp, angular and broken lines | Imprecise, varying shapes, usually triangles | Not filled completely, indicating a lack of patience |

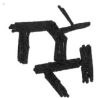 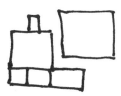

| ...erally thick, straight ...es full of presence | Rectangular or square shapes | Uniform filling, with clear, dark and precise borders |

7. Images

Our multi-levelled soul communicates with us through symbols and images. Since the time when humanity began to observe ourselves and the world, cultures have created endless views of the soul that have found expression in the creations of gods and adventure-packed myths. The Bible is rich with images and stories of legendary heroes confronted with situations that test their strength. Through these very human stories we learn about the many twisting fates and faces of the body and soul. According to the Old Testament, God created humanity in His image. The original Hebrew word (Tzelem) is not explicit. However, we learn from this that part of our structure is related to the supreme wisdom that created us. Jung called this divine particle the "Self". The Self is that place we aspire to reach; it is the unification with All That Is. All knowledge is hidden within the Self. To approach that divine light hidden within us, we must quiet the noises that prevent us from hearing our inner voice with clarity, and from observing and studying it. To help us in this circuitous communication, the Self sends messages through intuition. It is not a simple process to translate these messages. Our brain translates thoughts, emotions and memories as visual images associated with the world around us. This is especially notable in our dreams.

We can divide our perception of the world into the conscious and the unconscious. In the conscious, illuminated and revealed world, we act and create. The unconscious, dark and concealed realm is the source of our ideas, desires and decisions. According to Jungian theory, images from the unconscious that appear in our dreams have universal meanings in all cultures. Jung called these images "archetypes"; their meanings are part of the human collective unconscious. An egg, for example, is universally associated with the womb and birth.

The unconscious world is rich in images. While working on mandalas, the gates between the conscious and the unconscious open and heretofore hidden images and messages emerge. In mandala drawings, some images are very clear, while some images are only discerned after deep contemplation. When we begin to decipher the images, we begin with personal interpretations. After that, it is possible to relate to archetypal associations. Lastly, we combine all the comments to reach a final interpretation of the mandala.

I have collected a number of images that are frequently found in mandala drawings. These images come from the realm of animals, plants, the human body and celestial bodies.

Animals

Snake

The snake, crawling on its belly, represents the earth element and is associated with materiality and sensuality. The snake sheds its skin numerous times during its life and is frequently depicted swallowing its tail, all of which symbolize change, renewal, death and birth. Although snake venom can kill, it can also be used to create medicine and, as such, it is an ancient symbol of opposites: life and death, health and sickness. It represents the dark side of man, as well as divine wisdom. The snake is also a clear phallic symbol and represents male sexuality.

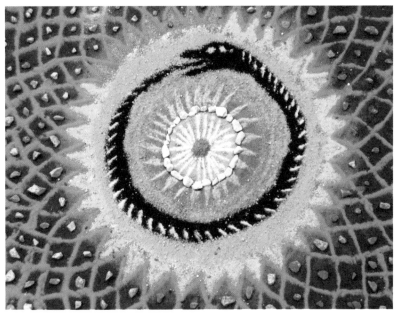

In Judaism, the snake is the first animal mentioned in the Bible. It is described as the creature that tempted Eve to taste the fruit of knowledge, which changed the fate of humanity. In the Book of Numbers, we are told that "Moses made a serpent of brass, and set it upon a pole; and it came to pass that if a serpent had bitten any man, when he looked unto the serpent of brass, he lived" (Numbers 21:9).

The brass serpent was preserved for many generations and displayed as a ritual object in the temple until it was destroyed by King Hezekiah. In ancient Egypt, a snake symbolizing the inner eye and power of rule decorated Pharaohs' crowns. According to Greek mythology, the world was created from a giant egg made of silver encircled by an ancient snake that symbolized the fire of the spirit of creation. The healing power of Asclepius, god of healing, was symbolized by a snake wrapped around a staff. This then became the known symbol of medicine and remains so to this day. Hermes, the messenger of the gods, carried a staff with two entwined snakes, representing life on earth and life of the dead in the underworld.

In many Eastern cultures, the snake represents kundalini energy, the life force residing at the base of the spine. When it is at rest, it is likened to a snake coiled up like a spring. In spiritual work, when this energy awakens, it rises up through the chakra centres, aspiring to unite with the crown chakra and experience wholeness and bliss.

Butterfly

The butterfly symbolizes our attitude toward freedom, ease and change. The butterfly undergoes amazing changes in its life cycle: from a crawling caterpillar to a cocooned chrysalis to a beautiful, colourful butterfly flying from flower to flower. It represents the human yearning to free the soul confined in the body. The butterfly's antennae represent communication with our surroundings. Thus, when we interpret the mandala, we should pay attention to any butterfly's direction, size and form. The delicate vulnerability of the butterfly represents the soul and its longing for unity, balance and harmony. Its spectacular colours and the symmetrical, two-sided structure of its wings represent our aspirations for perfect beauty. Butterflies look like they are dancing when they fly over the flowers, awakening within us feelings of lightness and joy. In early Christianity, the butterfly symbolized the soul. In China, it is considered the symbol of the union of bliss and joy, and people in India see it as a symbol of transformation and joy.

In mandalas we find two main types of butterflies. One is a butterfly moving freely, without limitations, for example, a butterfly in an open space in the upper section of the mandala. The second is a butterfly imprisoned within a framework, representing the desire to move, to be free and to spread its wings.

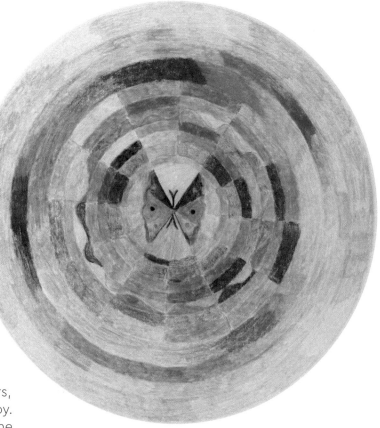

Fish

The fish lives in water and thus represents the water element and the emotions. The silence of the fish represents the desire for verbal emotional expression. The fish also represents female fertility, health, abundance and good luck. For early Christians, fish symbolized Jesus, since the Greek word for fish – ichthys – was an acrostic for the words "Jesus Christ God's Son Savior". Many folktales tell of fish swallowing precious gems in the deep sea, later found by fishermen. The fish represents the ability to dive to unknown places in the depths of the soul and to return with life-changing messages and treasures.

Eagle

The eagle is considered the king of the birds and ruler of the skies. It represents the element of air and wisdom. The eagle has a wide wingspan and an ability to soar effortlessly for long periods of time. Its impressive flying abilities represent our ability to see things from above and to discern structures and processes. The eagle frequently appears as a white eagle, symbolizing pure, unbiased vision. Among the Pueblo people, the eagle was a symbol of purity. Eagles appearing in a mandala can represent strength, power, healing, control over situations, victory, success, knowledge, understanding, guidance and spiritual direction.

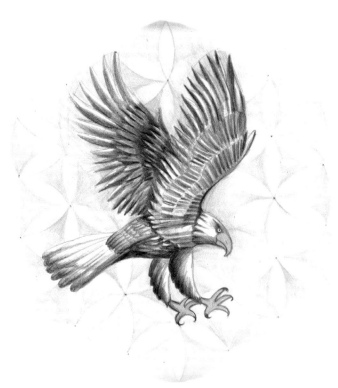

Plants

Tree

The tree represents the cycles of life, a journey that begins with a seed, becomes a soft sapling and grows into a tree that bears fruits with new seeds, and so on and so forth. The tree symbolizes both the hidden and the revealed. The source of life is in the roots deep within the earth. The deeper the tree's roots, the more stable the trunk will be in changing weather. Similarly, a person can withstand the hardships of life when their spiritual, material and social roots are deep. Like handwriting, a drawing of a tree expresses the personality of the person doing the drawing. As such, a psychological diagnostic theory has been built around tree paintings.

In the Old Testament, there are many comparisons made between a man and a tree: "For the tree of the field is man's life" (Deuteronomy 20:19); "For he shall be as a tree planted by the water" (Jeremiah 17:8). The Tree of Knowledge and the Tree of Life figure prominently in the Garden of Eden story. According to the Kabbalah, the Tree of Life describes the structure of the universe and the connection between humanity and God. According to Jung, the tree represents the Self and humanity's need to grow and be filled with the divine presence.

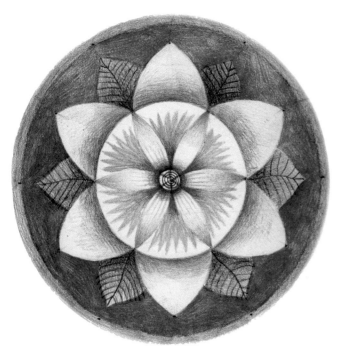

Flower

Many flowers look like a natural mandala, with petals surrounding the centre. The flower is one stage in the life of a plant. It symbolizes the spring, youthful blossoming, sexual maturity and fertility. It also symbolizes opening the gateways to the processes of growth and development. It appears as an expression of beauty and love at ceremonies marking significant milestones: births, marriages and funerals.

Flowers have received different meanings in different cultures. The rose can symbolize love, passion or death. The white lily represents purity and virginity. The lily is for birth, awe of God and humility. The gladiolus in Mexico represents death. In the East, the lotus symbolizes humanity's aspiration for enlightenment. Its roots are in the earth, it grows in water and its flowers open in the air to divine light.

Pomegranate

The ripe, red pomegranate represents wisdom and actualizing the knowledge of maturity. The pomegranate is reminiscent of the womb and birth canal. Like an idea that has reached the time for its fruition, so the seeds are ripe to see the light of the world and grow as new trees. In many societies around the world, it is customary to adorn a bride with pomegranate fruit and leaves on her wedding day as a symbol of fertility. The crown on the pomegranate represents the connection to the higher self and pure divine thought. The pomegranate is one of the "seven kinds" of crops that the land of Israel was blessed with (Deuteronomy 8:8). In Judaism it is a symbol for beauty, wisdom and abundance. According to Jewish tradition, a pomegranate has 613 seeds, comparable to the 613 Torah commandments (Mitzvoth) that we are supposed to fulfill. A pomegranate is traditionally eaten at the Rosh HaShana (Jewish New Year) dinner while saying the blessing, "May our merits increase like the seeds of a pomegranate". Silver and brass pomegranates embellish the Torah scrolls and symbolize the Tree of Life.

In ancient Egypt the pharaohs customarily stored pomegranates in their coffins to ensure a safe transition to the next word. Another myth from the ancient world is from Greek mythology: Hades kidnapped Persephone, the beautiful daughter of the Goddess of the Earth, Demeter, and brought her to his kingdom in the underworld. Persephone unwittingly ate a number of pomegranate seeds from the kitchen of the underworld king, thus sealing her fate to be imprisoned in the underworld for one-third of every year.

In the Quran, the pomegranate is referred to as the fruit of the Garden of Eden, whereas Christian icon painters placed a pomegranate in Jesus's hand as a symbol of sacredness.

Tendrils

Tendrils are curling stems that grow from the base of the leaf on climbing plants to help the plant attach to its environment. The shape of the curled tendril looks like a spiral and suggests rapid awakening, development and growth. The movement radiates positive energy. It is a soft, feminine, containing, flowing and rounded movement. The shape of the tendril is very decorative and prevalent in the decorative arts in many cultures.

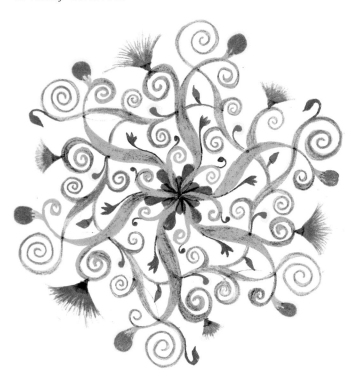

The Human Body

Eyes

We experience the world through our eyes. The eye's shape reminds us of a mandala with the pupil as the centre, the bindu. Open eyes symbolize wakefulness and the revealed, while closed eyes symbolize sleep, dreams and the hidden. Seeing connects to the aspiration for clarity and awareness, whereas closed eyes symbolize turning inwards and inner contemplation. The eye is the archetype representing both inner observation and a sense of criticism from outside.

Cultures and mythologies worldwide connect blindness with extrasensory perception and prophecy. The blind are not tempted by outer appearances and are able to see a person's inner soul. The ability of the blind to see the secrets of the soul symbolizes truth and justice. In Greek mythology, for example, blind Tiresias succeeded in prophesizing the future of the heroes.

When deciphering a mandala:

- Light coloured eyes – openness and self-expression
- Red or orange eyes – criticism, connection to the root chakra
- Eyelashes – eyes open and seeing
- No eyelashes – judgmental
- Eye angled vertically – judgmental
- Eye angled horizontally – opening
- Prominent pupil – opening
- Eye without a pupil – judgmental
- Many eyes – "I am being looked at and I have to please others". Alternatively, "I am excited and contemplating life".

Hand

Hands are the body part that enables us to actualize our desires and aspirations. The hand symbolizes doing. Hands can receive and give. The hand-shaped hamsa amulet signifies good luck.

Hand movements are used as a language for communication. Waving hello, for example, is always with an open hand, suggesting pure intentions. The fist, on the other hand, connotes struggle and concealment. The signing language for the deaf is based on hand movements.

In Hindu culture, hand positions called mudras are used to communicate. In paintings portraying Buddha, for example, the position of his hands expresses compassion and love.

Heart

The heart represents blood, feelings and the soul. It expresses our ability to give and receive love.

In the past, before scientists identified the brain as the control centre for all the organs, various qualities were attributed to the heart because death was determined at the moment the heart stopped beating. Many ceremonies expressed this belief. For example, the Aztecs sacrificed the hearts of prisoners to the god of the sun.

The heart signifies the centre of the body and soul. The hands on both sides serve to give and receive from the heart. Many linguistic phrases that contain the word "heart" express our emotional attitude to the world, such as: "to take to heart", "to put your heart into something", "to give from the heart", etc. In Western society, the symbol of the red heart is an expression of love.

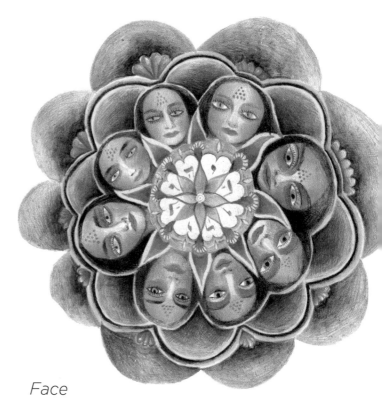

Face

A person's face is a sensitive and complex tool for expressing emotions. Contracted facial expressions generally connote fear, anger and aggression. Open facial expressions symbolize joy, openness and pleasure. The face is a basic tool of communication, beginning from infancy. Any facial feature can appear in a mandala drawing in different shapes, angles and sizes.

Detailed facial features in a mandala signify a deepening of the personal story and the willingness to go into greater depth. Figures that appear without facial features are generally symbolic. Various cultures use masks with exaggerated facial expressions at holidays and ceremonies; for example, Indian ceremonies, the carnival in Venice, All Saints Day or Halloween in Christianity and Purim in Judaism.

Celestial Bodies

Sun

From earliest times, when our ancestors hunted and gathered, the sun has symbolized daylight, activity and awareness.

The round sun looks like a mandala. It is the source of life. The warm sunlight represents the fire element, the power that connects wisdom to creation. In Western society, the sun is the archetype of the father figure. It represents the masculine, the revealed, the initiator and the active.

Drawing the sun connects us to the characteristics of self-control, the power of leadership and direction. The sun's rays denote masculine movement that moves like an arrow with aimed focus. The sun symbolizes our head. The head is the locus of consciousness and, from there, commands are transmitted to the rest of the body. Just as we can't see our heads directly, but only through a mirror, so we can't look directly at the sun, but view it through its reflected rays. This is similar to the divine essence in the world. We can't experience God directly but only through observation of His actions, revealed in creation.

In Greek mythology, the sun god, Helios, is described as riding on a chariot harnessed to four horses, symbolizing dominion over the four cardinal directions, north, south, east and west. We can see the image of the sun god in the Beit Alpha synagogue mosaic, depicting the zodiac with Helios, the sun god, in the centre.

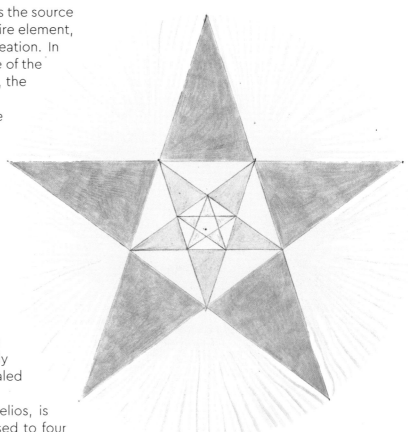

Moon

The moon circles the earth on a monthly cycle and its appearance changes every night. In many mythologies around the world, the moon symbolizes the night while we are sleeping and dreaming. The moon also symbolizes changes in our emotional body that, like a pendulum, swings from joyful fullness to miserable emptiness.

The cyclical nature of the moon symbolizes the feminine cycles. In ancient tribes and traditions, women developed calendars and ceremonies according to the moon in which men were forbidden to take part. The moon is connected to the element of water that melts and clouds boundaries. It represents night, dreams, feminine wisdom, extra-sensory perception and that which is hidden from view. The moon reflects the sun's light and is not a source of light itself. As such, it symbolizes the feminine ability to contain and receive.

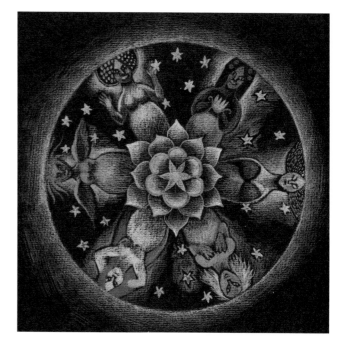

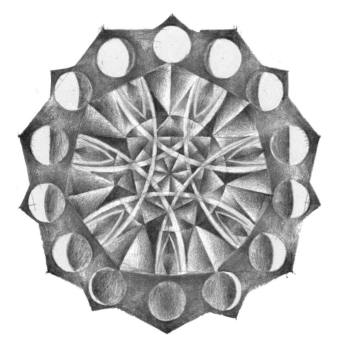

Star

The night sky looks like a huge, round bowl filled with dots of light. In the Book of the Zohar, the stars are described as holes in the blanket of the sky that let us peek at the divine light behind the veil. They represent support, optimism and hope that reach us from afar. On the other hand, in a mandala they frequently indicate secondary circles in our lives, for example, siblings and friends. Thus in the Old Testament story in which young Joseph dreamed that his family bowed before him, Jacob, his father, was seen as the sun, his mother as the moon and his brothers as the stars.

It is different when we discern one large star painted in a mandala, especially in its centre. Such a star signifies star dust, illusions of the world of glamour and the need to be filled by external admiration.

Rainbow

The curving rainbow in the sky is a symbol of freedom, openness and the connection between humanity, spirituality and the divine.

The rainbow is a refraction of white light into seven colours. Each colour represents another part of human existence. The white, for instance, symbolizes the divine element within human existence. The combination of colours represents human variation and unity.

In the Old Testament story of Noah, the rainbow symbolizes a covenant of peace between God and humanity. In the mandala, the rainbow symbolizes a sense of unity and a broad view of all possibilities. It can also indicate searching, confusion and a lack of focus.

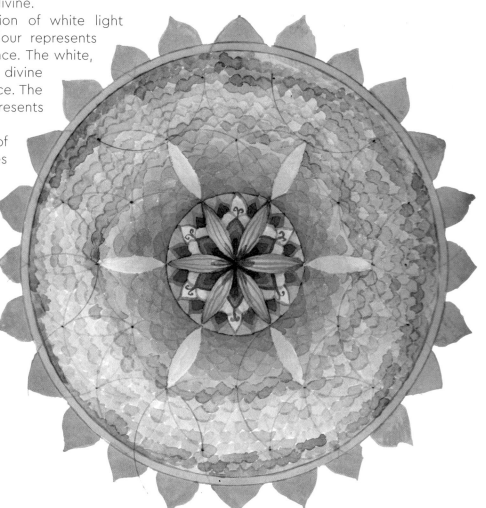

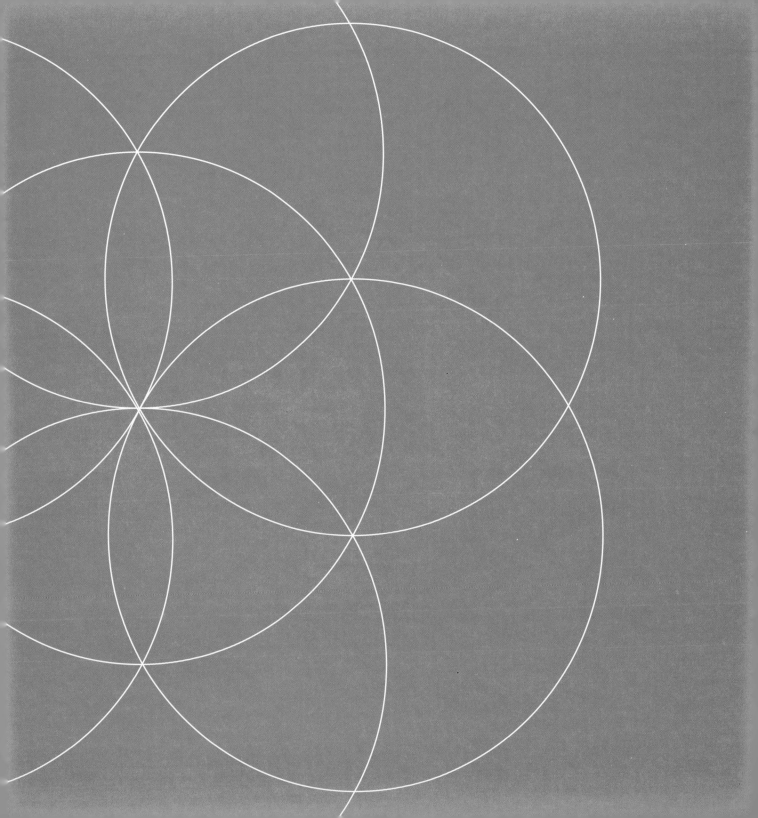

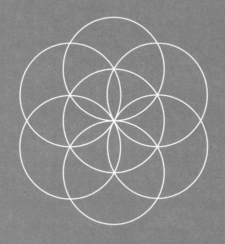

PART TWO
HOW TO DRAW MANDALAS

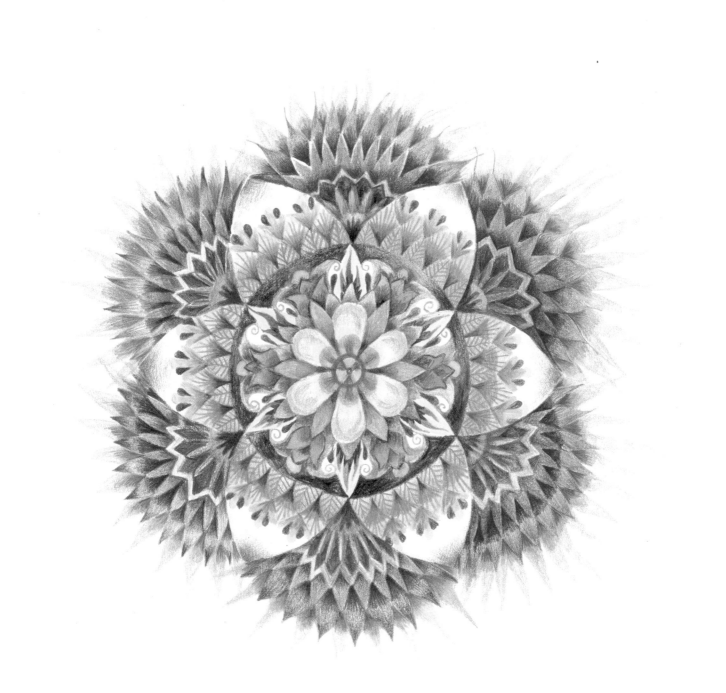

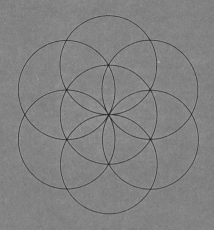

1

SEED OF LIFE MANDALA
THE ORDER OF CREATION

What is the hidden spring within me that wishes to manifest in the world?
Where is creativity present in my life?
How am I reborn each moment, here and now?

The History of the Seed of Life Mandala

The Seed of Life pattern is a geometric shape made from seven equal-sized circles. This pattern is found in various cultures. It is etched on the concealed inner walls of Egypt's pyramids and on mythological animal statues of ancient China. It also served as a decorative motif on burial caskets of members of the nobility in ancient Greece and Rome. The meaning of the Seed of Life mandala is creation, beginnings, birth and primacy. The shape contains the mathematical and geometrical basis of everything that exists: light, colour, sound, shape, magnetic fields and molecular bodies. The format is composed of interwoven circles, within which are concealed all existing geometric shapes. There are even those who claim that the secrets of creation are hidden there.

In the process of creating the mandala, we reenact the process of creation as told in various mythologies throughout the world. According to the Old Testament, God created the world in six days and on the seventh day He rested and enjoyed and observed what He had created. Similarly, in the Seed of Life mandala, six circles form around the seventh and, within it, a flower blooms. The first circle creates something from nothing. After its creation, the circle repeats itself to create infinite combinations out of the initial shape.

The first circle, analogous to the Big Bang theory in physics, explains the creation of the world. According to this theory, the source of the universe is a single point called "gravitational singularity". The Big Bang describes a formative event that happened 14 billion years ago when the universe, the dimension of time and all the spatial and physical dimensions came into being. Over time, the universe expanded to the dimensions known today, and each point has its source in the Big Bang. In 1929, Edwin Hubble, the American astronomer, discovered that the galaxies are becoming more and more distant from each other, contributing to the theory that the universe is expanding.

In our souls there are infinite hidden occurrences waiting to reveal themselves. To begin a creative act, we go through a process of choosing one of infinite possibilities that are waiting to manifest in the world. A similar process underlies the secrets of the Kabbalah, called tzimtzum (contraction, constriction). God, who filled the world, constricted His presence so that the world could be created. In his Kabbalistic teachings, Rabbi Isaac Luria speaks of the principle of tzimtzum: "and when God decided to create the worlds...to manifest the perfection of His actions, names and appellations, which was the reason for creating the worlds. And so God infinitely contracted Himself to a central point, which was right in the middle...and He removed Himself to the sides around the central point... and this contraction...around the empty central point was circular all around." Thus, because of the contraction of the divine light, an empty space was created that was able to contain all the upper and lower worlds. The shape of the space that was formed was circular, without dimensions.

The Seed of Life mandala lets us take part in a process of birth and beginning, and so increases our curiosity and never-ending renewal. It teaches us to look at the events in our life with fresh eyes, like a newborn, seeing the world for the first time and experiencing the thrill of discovery. The mandala enables us to connect to the essence of life, growth and continual creation and change. This is the mother of all mandalas, and all the other mandalas derive from it. Drawing this mandala helps to free the creativity within, move forward when we are blocked, find solutions to problems. It releases pain rooted in the past, cleanses, renews, reorganizes and empowers our life force and the desire to discover the world and to create.

Stages in Creating the Seed of Life Mandala

1. Chaos

We begin the process by contemplating the sheet of white paper. Look at the paper and return to a time before the world was created. On the white paper there are infinite points from which we can start to draw the mandala. Thinking about the infinite possibilities that existed prior to the creation of the world, we awaken the creativity that exists within us.

2. Contraction and Choice

Placing the compass point in the centre of the white page represents choice. From all the infinite potentials, we choose one point. The moment of choice is the moment we fix the compass point on the page. At this moment we forego all other possibilities. The centre point – the bindu – opens the gate between the concealed world and the revealed world; now what was previously only an idea can manifest. Just as the infinite God constricted himself to create a world, by drawing the mandala we enable one of the infinite potentials to manifest.

3. The Big Bang

From the point of choice, the first circle is created around the bindu. At this stage, we start to create something from nothing, just like in the Big Bang theory. We serve as a channel that makes it possible for creation to manifest through us. We need only to devote ourselves to the process of growth and development and our creation will burst forth into the material world quite naturally.

4. The Six Days of Creation

The circle is divided into six equal parts by duplicating the circle around the first circle, similar to the six days of creation. The central circle, in which a flower has been formed, is analogous to the Sabbath, the seventh day. According to numerology, the occult meaning of numbers, six signifies wholeness, harmony and the beauty of creation. The Old Testament begins with the Hebrew word B'resheet which means "in the beginning". (The Aramaic word is Bara shesh or "created six".) When water freezes, amazingly beautiful hexagonal crystals are formed, reminding us of the Seed of Life mandala based on the number six.

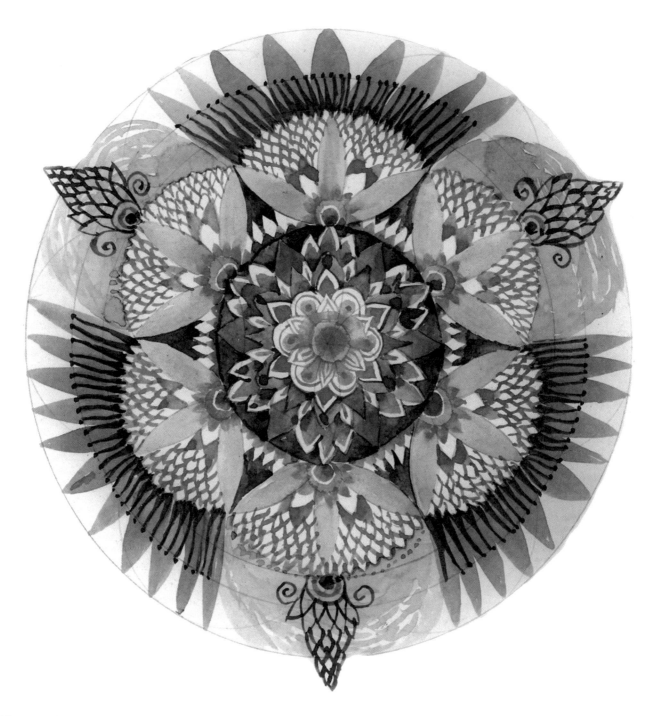

Seed of Life Meditation

Sit in a comfortable position on a chair or pillow; make sure your spine is erect but relaxed. Imagine a ring connected to a taut string at the crown of your head pulling your spine upward, creating space, letting your lungs open wide. Close your eyes and focus on your breathing. Air enters, air exits. With each exhale, release all the tension in your body. Take seven deep breaths. Concentrate on the air that enters and exits your body. Tightly tense the muscles of your eyes, lips, shoulders, arms, hands, buttocks, abdomen, legs and feet. Then relax each body part, one after the other. Repeat this tensing and relaxing.

There are many sources of creativity within you desiring to manifest in the world. They are like underground springs waiting to be tapped. Intuitively identify a place in your body that wants to feel the touch of your hands, and place one hand on top of the other in that place. It can be anywhere on your body: legs, feet, stomach, head, etc. Trust your hands to take you to the right place. Once you have placed your focus on a particular area, see it as the bindu of the mandala, the place from which you want to give birth to your creative potential. Now imagine how removing a rock covering a spring's source allows the stream of bubbling water to flow forth freely. The placement of your hands identifies the point from which your creative potential flows forth at this moment. You can feel the release that this flowing feeling brings. From the bindu point you are born anew.

Slowly, return to the feeling of here and now and open your eyes. Move on to the drawing of the mandala.

HOW TO DRAW THE MANDALA

① Open the compass to a radius of 3.5cm (1½in) and place the compass point on the centre of the page.

② Draw a circle around this point.

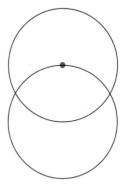

③ Place the compass point at the top of the circle you have just drawn and draw a second circle using the same radius.

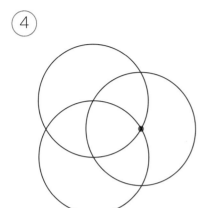

(4)

Make a third circle whose
centre is the right intersection
point of the first two circles.

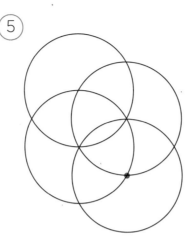

(5)

Make a fourth circle from the
third intersection point.

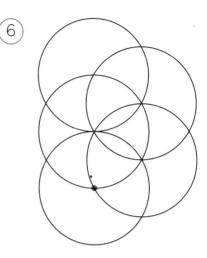

(6)

Move to the next
intersection point and make
a circle from here.

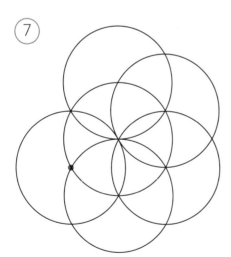

(7)

Once again, move to the
next intersection point and
make a circle.

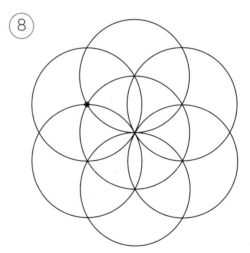

(8)

Finally, make a circle from
the next intersection point,
completing the template.

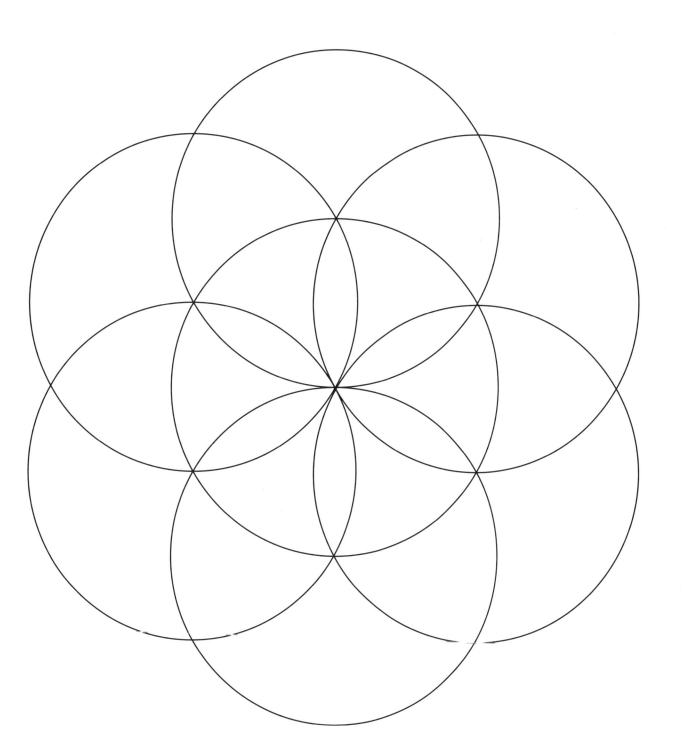

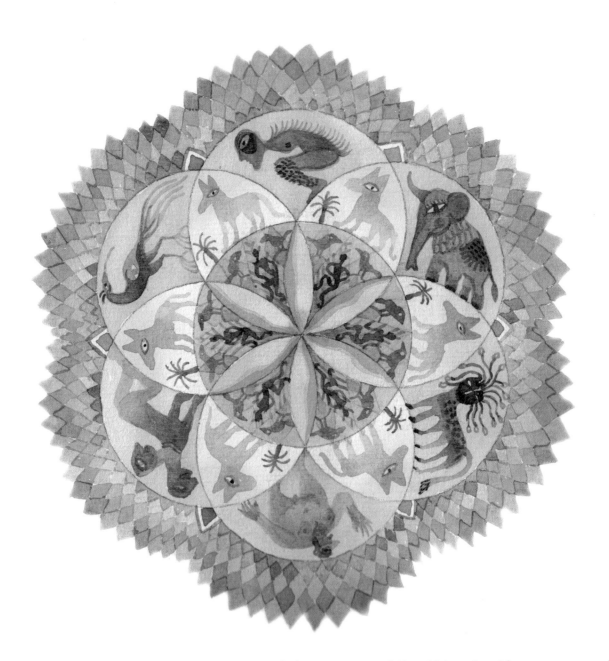

A journey in the inner world of fairytales: Creation of a harmonious world in which real and fantasy creatures live together. The watercolours create a gentle transparency that adds to the feeling of quiet and tranquility.

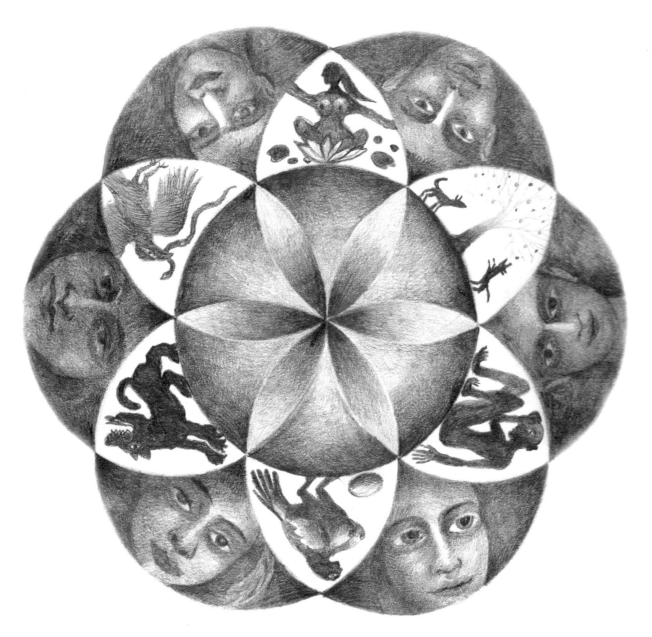

This pencil drawing has a wide range of shading, from dark to light. In the centre circle are only geometric shapes. The second circle has archetypal figures that combine imaginary and realistic elements, and the third circle has realistically drawn figures. The three circles signify three developmental stages in our understanding of the inner and outer world.

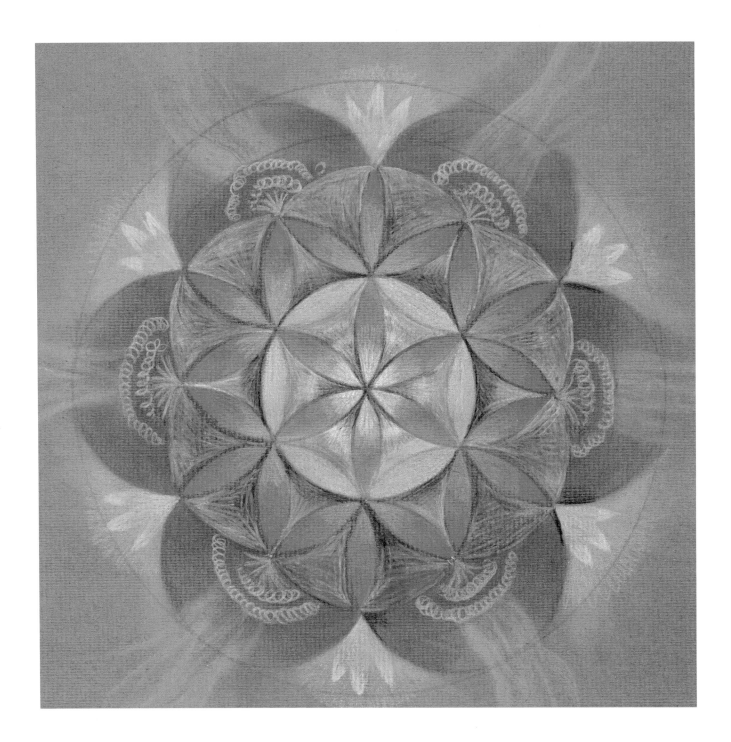

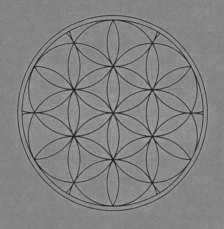

2
FLOWER OF LIFE MANDALA
INFINITE SPACE

How do I allow myself to be in a world of infinite space?
Who am I and what is my unique path in the world?
How do I walk courageously over the narrow bridge of life?

The History of the Flower of Life Mandala

The creation of the world is symbolized by the Seed of Life – a pattern of seven connected circles. After the creation, the world continues to expand at every moment. Even this moment, in which you are reading this book, is a unique moment that has just been created; there has never been a moment like it before. The Flower of Life describes a huge world that unfolds before us at every step, a world that grows endlessly. From the six circles that surround the first circle in the Seed of Life, more and more circles are collected, and we get an infinite pattern. Through the Flower of Life, we understand the essence of life.

The Flower of Life template looks like a huge field of six-petalled flowers. According to ancient wisdom, the Flower of Life contains everything that has ever been created. This image represents all the languages, mathematical formulas, laws of physics, musical harmonies and biological forms, including the human body. The Flower of Life pattern was found carved on a column in the temple of the Egyptian god of the dead, Osiris, dated to 6,000 years ago. It is also seen in ancient and modern designs and on artifacts found across the world, including Ireland, Turkey, Britain, China, Greece, Japan and Israel. Throughout history, philosophers, artists and architects have used this form to represent wholeness and harmony in their work. Leonardo da Vinci seriously investigated this pattern, as documented in many pages of his scientific drawings. In Israel, archaeologists found this symbol on an ancient sarcophagus inscribed with the name Yehoshua ben Yosef – Jesus, son of Joseph.

The Flower of Life appears as a simple design, but it hides cosmic knowledge within itself. The structure of the Kabbalah's Tree of Life is also derived from the Flower of Life template. The structure contains ten sephirot (attributes) and 22 pathways that interconnect. According to the Kabbalah, the Tree of Life depicts the structure of all creation.

The Flower of Life symbolizes primordial creation. It represents the unlimited possibilities that are found within us, and the possibility to choose among them. While painting the Flower of Life mandala, imagine a multi-dimensional world full of unlimited possibilities and directions. Then, using your internal compass, choose the path that is uniquely yours.

A well-known phrase by Reb Nachman of Bratslav, the founder of the Hasidic movement, says, "All the world is a very narrow bridge, but the main thing is to have no fear at all." He meant that in life, one has endless choices, but the way is a narrow bridge that connects birth to death, where we should walk safely in faith, without fear. The Flower of Life pattern allows us to practice our ability to choose the right way at any junction we reach. The source of a good choice comes from the connection to the central point, the bindu, where we experience the source of the soul. We ask ourselves while creating the mandala: what colour or shape is right for me at this moment? The mandala grows from stage to stage in choices that stem from the inner essence, and the belief in our ability to make the right choices grows. The Flower of Life painting reinforces the belief that the right answers to any questions or worries are within us.

When we draw the Flower of Life mandala, we allow ourselves to release tension and distress. The mandala helps us to focus on our own unique path and make decisions from that place. It teaches us to navigate between freedom and limitations and helps us to feel connected to the universe and people in the world.

Flower of Life Meditation

Sit in a comfortable position on a chair or pillow; make sure your spine is erect but relaxed. Imagine a ring connected to a taut string at the crown of your head pulling your spine upward, creating space, letting your lungs open wide. Close your eyes and focus on your breathing. Air enters, air exits. With each exhale, release all the tension in your body. Take seven deep breaths. Concentrate on the air that enters and exits your body. Tightly tense the muscles of your eyes, lips, shoulders, arms, hands, buttocks, abdomen, legs and feet. Then relax each body part, one after the other. Repeat this tensing and relaxing.

Identify within your body the point that embodies the centre of the mandala, the bindu. This place is asking you for more attention and increased energy.

Find the part of your body suitable for you today, and place your hands there, one on top of the other. Any place on the body can be chosen; trust your hands to lead you to the right place at this time.

Imagine a small but intense beam of light centred in this spot. It expands and grows with energy that comes through your breathing and your hands. This ball of light grows in stages. At first it fills your body. It then expands to fill the room, then the city you are living in, then the country and finally the whole world.

Stay for a while with the feeling of fullness that the ball of light has brought you; feel that you are one with the world. Then gradually contract the light back to the bindu point from where it began to expand.

Slowly, return to the feeling of here and now and open your eyes. Move on to the drawing of the mandala.

HOW TO DRAW THE MANDALA

①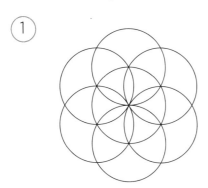

Open the compass to a radius of 3.5cm (1½in) and draw the Seed of Life template as described in Lesson 1 (page 57).

②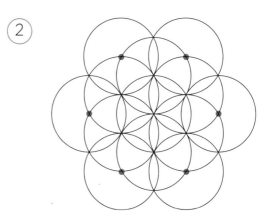

Mark the six intersection points of the six circles with a pencil and, using the same radius, draw a circle at each marked point.

③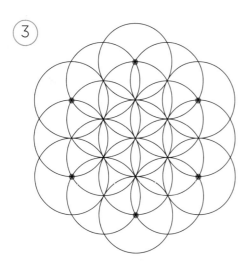

Mark the six new intersection points with a pencil and draw a circle at each marked point.

④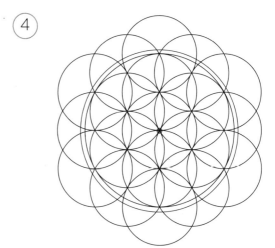

Draw two large circles, 0.5cm (¼in) distance from one another, to circumscribe the circles drawn. You might want to erase the lines outside of these two large circles.

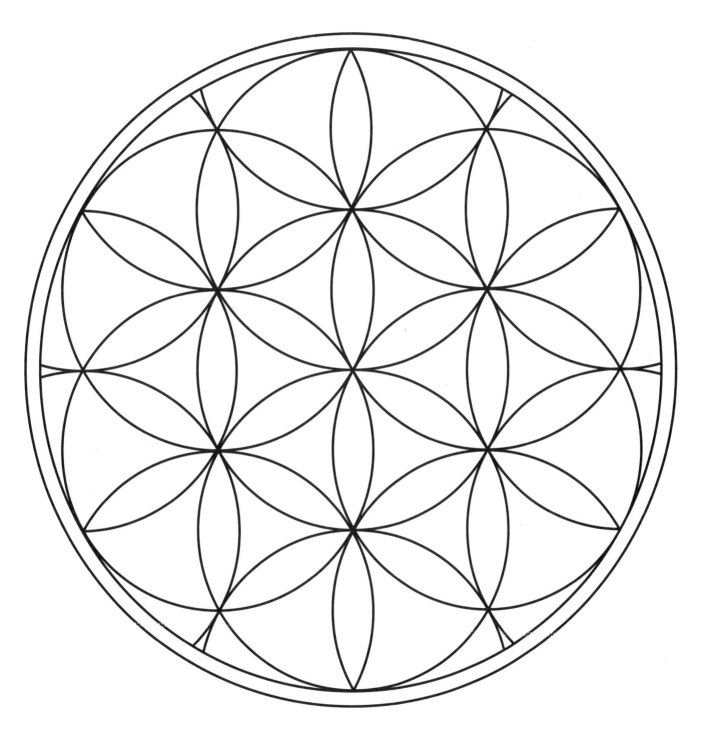

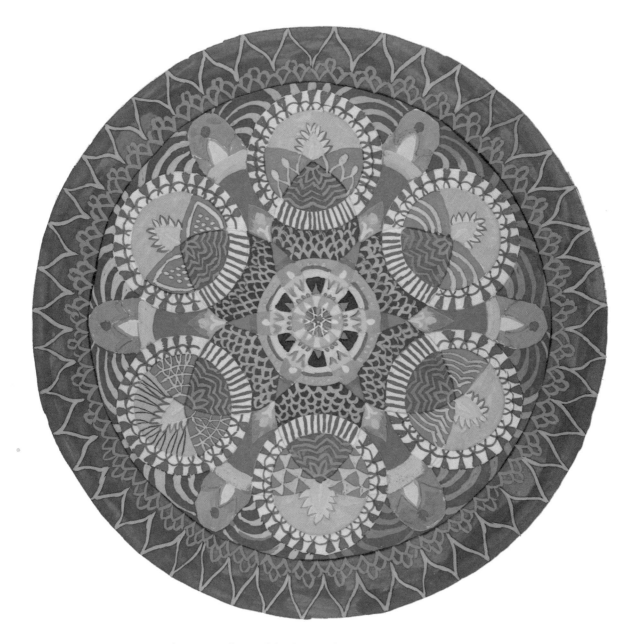

A gouache painted mandala that, at first glance, looks symmetrical.
In fact, in each one of its parts there are different details, revealing hidden worlds.

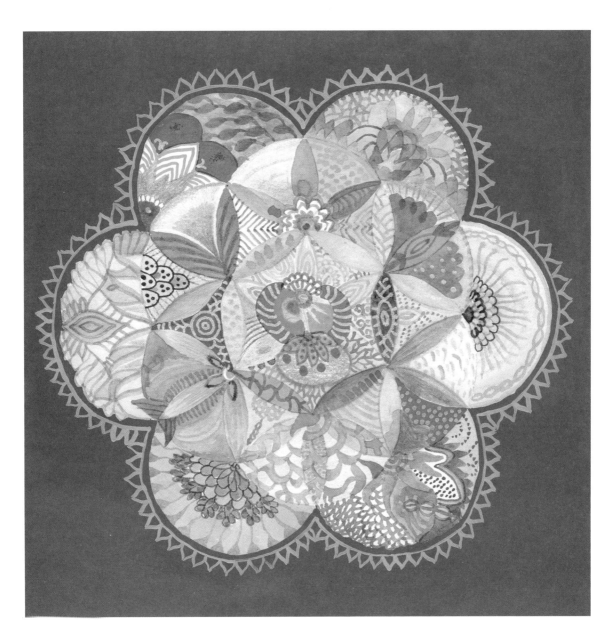

A watercolour mandala takes us on a journey through different landscapes.
True freedom means choice and a new possibility at every moment.

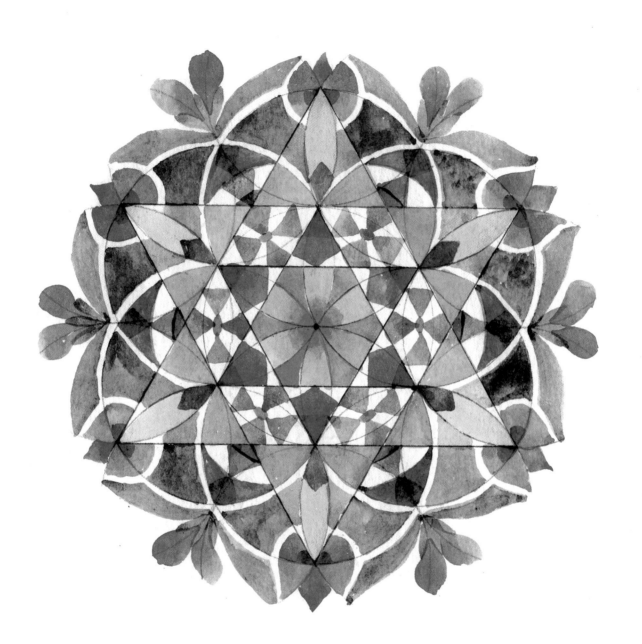

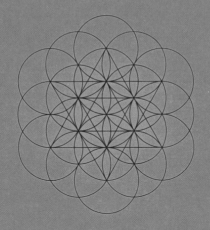

3
YANTRA MANDALA
THE UNITY OF OPPOSITES

What are the masculine and feminine parts within me?
How do I balance the polarities and opposites within me?
How can I reconcile my independent self with the wholeness of a couple?

The History of the Yantra Mandala

The word "yantra" is a combination of two Sanskrit words: "yan", meaning instrument or tool, and "tra", meaning liberation or release. In Buddhist tradition this refers to the tool for release from the cycle of birth and death.

The yantra is used as a visual focus in meditation. It embodies symbolic depictions of divine entities which represent aspects of reality. Drawing a yantra requires a great deal of precision, discipline, concentration and patience; the essence of the triangle is focus and concentration of energy.

There are many yantras, but the most important one is the Shri Yantra. In Sanskrit, Shri is the name of the goddess of the earth. This yantra is dedicated to the divine mother and symbolizes creation of the world. The Shri Yantra is built from the intersections of nine equilateral triangles, five facing opward and four facing downwards. The five triangles with their apexes opward belong to the masculine god, Shiva, and express the power of growth and development; in contrast, the four triangles facing downwards belong to the feminine goddess, Shakti, and express the power of dismantling and destruction. Their joining creates 43 smaller triangles which are related to the energy of the sun.

The centre point represents the seed of the entire universe and, in the human body, the sixth chakra, located between the eyes. Each detail of the Shri Yantra has symbolic meaning. For example, the two rings around the centre are decorated with lotus leaves, which are associated with lunar energy and the realization of our wishes and aspirations. The Shri Yantra has a positive influence on health, abundance, success and improving interpersonal relationships. Contemplating it brings tranquility and harmony.

Triangles and pyramids are associated with pain relief, protection from negative energies, serenity and confidence. The combination of triangles in the Shri Yantra also create smaller mandalas, each with a different meaning. In the ancient world, triangles were used to denote the four elements. Fire and air were denoted by a triangle whose base is toward the ground, and water and earth by a triangle with its base in the air.

According to the Old Testament, God declared to his angels, "Let us make mankind in our image, after our likeness" (Genesis 1:26). Thus, the divine presence is found in each of us, and it is for us to connect to this spark of divinity within ourselves and activate it. This means taking full responsibility for our life and improving it to the best of our ability by connecting to our higher self.

In the Jewish tradition, the Star of David symbolizes the unity of opposites. The opposing triangles symbolize the polarity of feminine and masculine, which are perceived as complementary opposites. Masculine characteristics include decisiveness, analytical skills, dominance, aggressiveness, ambition, power, self-confidence and competitiveness. Feminine qualities include empathy, holistic contemplation, interest in the wellbeing of others, support skills, containment, caring, serenity and gentleness. I want to emphasize that gender characteristics do not originate from biological differences between the two sexes. Masculine and feminine qualities are found in both men and women to different degrees.

According to Indian symbolism, the triangle facing downwards embodies the feminine energy, called yoni, and the triangle facing opward expresses the masculine energy, called lingam. In Western tradition, the interpretation is opposite, with the bottom triangle representing the feminine principle and the upper triangle signifying the masculine. In Hinduism, the Star of David symbolizes the heart chakra. Located in the centre, it links the three more spiritual upper chakras and the three more earthly lower chakras.

When we draw the Star of David, using a ruler for precise straight lines and the compass for soft curving circles, we combine the linear masculine energy with the womb-like feminine energy. These essential differences can be seen in Jewish marriage customs. During the marriage ceremony under the canopy, the bride walks around the groom seven times. The woman, the rounded feminine essence, experiences reality from a multi-dimensional perspective, whereas the male's role is to be a straight line, a supportive axis for the wheel of femininity. An encounter between the masculine and the feminine often arises while drawing this mandala, allowing us to observe and contemplate how we respond to these aspects within ourselves.

The Bible tells how the male, created first, felt great loneliness and found no comfort among the animals. After he fell asleep, a rib was taken from him to create woman to be his helpmate. In drawing the Yantra mandala, in which we create angular shapes, representing the masculine, inside a circle, representing the feminine, we discover that it is the man who is born from the female.

Sometimes during the drawing process, women reflect on significant men in their lives – their father, husband, son or brother – and men think about the nature of their masculinity. The father archetype also signifies education and our relationship to the outside world. Consequently, our treatment of the lines and sharp angles of the Star of David can shed light on our relationship to authority and those figures that influenced our understanding of social behaviour. Accordingly, as we work on the Star of David pattern, we can reflect on our personal reaction to rules, authority and constraints, and we can examine if they raise feelings of suffocation or give us a sense of protection, confidence and a framework for action.

Words related to the masculine essence are: memory, axis, goal, sun, ruler, day, external, action, source of light and warmth, activity, line.

Words related to the feminine essence are: experience, horizon, moon, compass, night, internal, intuition, acceptance, passivity, softness.

Star of David Meditation

Sit in a comfortable position on a chair or pillow; make sure your spine is erect but relaxed. Imagine a ring connected to a taut string at the crown of your head pulling your spine upward, creating space, letting your lungs open wide. Close your eyes and focus on your breathing. Air enters, air exits. With each exhale, release all the tension in your body. Take seven deep breaths. Concentrate on the air that enters and exits your body. Tightly tense the muscles of your eyes, lips, shoulders, arms, hands, buttocks, abdomen, legs and feet. Then relax each body part, one after the other. Repeat this tensing and relaxing.

While breathing deeply and quietly, examine the balance between the right and left sides of your body. Try to feel a balance between the left and right sides for all your bodily pairs, external and internal, like the left brain versus the right brain, the eyes, shoulders, arms, legs. If the right side seems heavier, dominant or stronger, use your imagination to transfer energy to the other side, until a feeling of balance is achieved.

Stay for a while with this feeling of balance between the right and left; experience the feeling of calm between the two poles.

Slowly, return to the feeling of here and now, and open your eyes. Move on to the drawing of the mandala.

HOW TO DRAW THE MANDALA

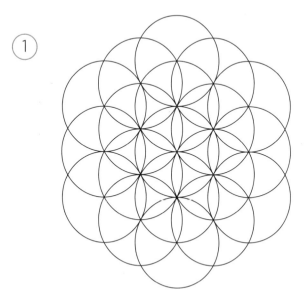

① Open the compass to a radius of 3.5cm (1½in) and draw the Flower of Life mandala as described in Lesson 2 (page 67).

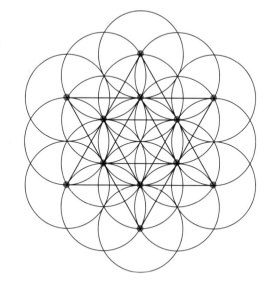

② Mark the 12 intersection points, as shown, and using a pencil and ruler, draw lines connecting the intersection points.

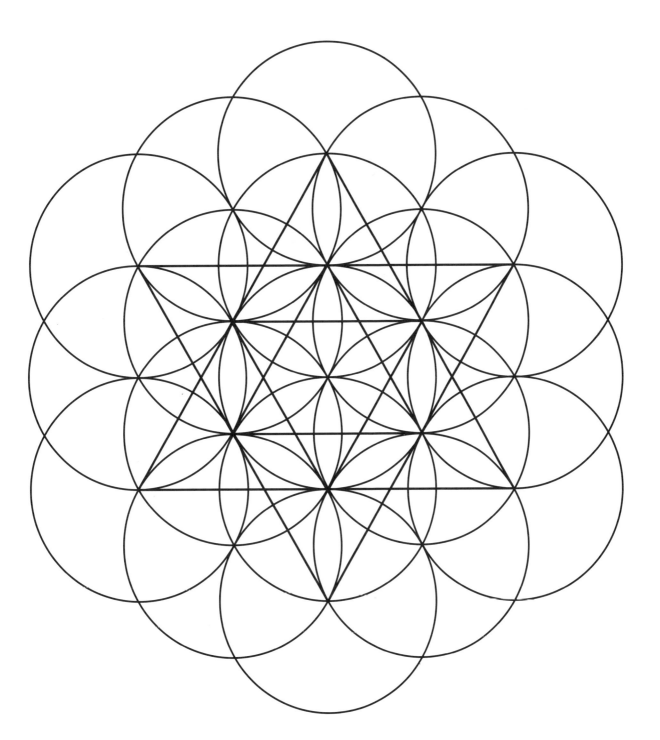

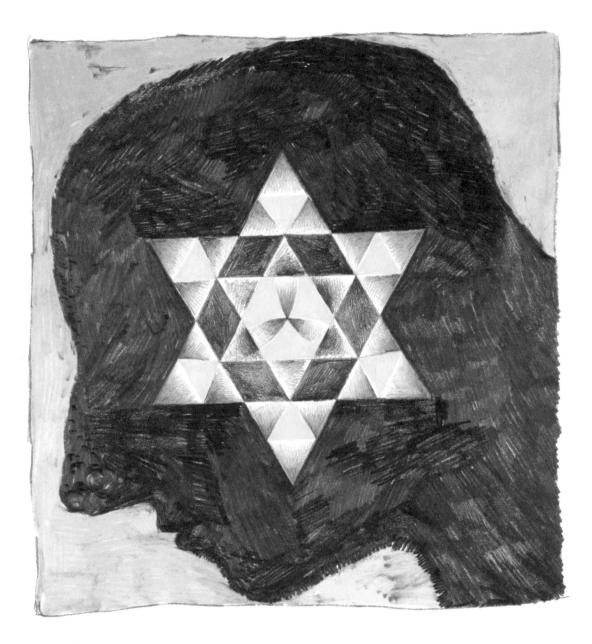

A mandala in the form of the Star of David placed in the head of the shaded figure represents consciousness and thought. The use of pencil reveals expressive strokes of the hand. The figure personifies the darkness within us. The choice of yellow emphasizes a feeling of distress.

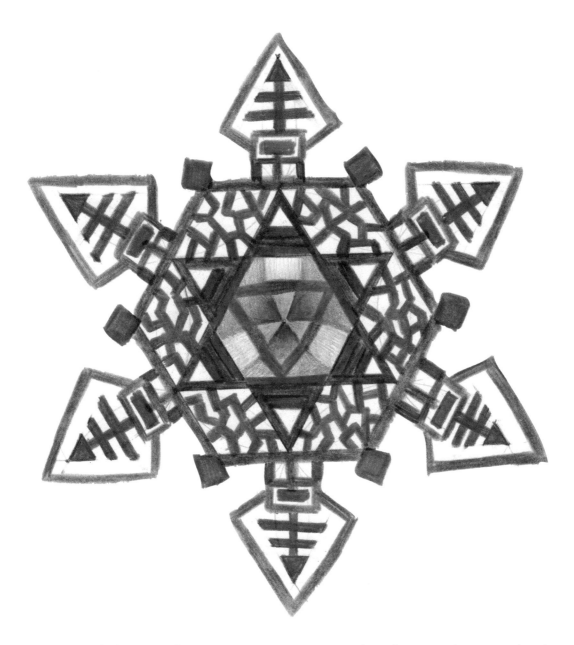

The sharp triangles symbolize masculine aggressiveness protecting the softer internal areas. Red and green are complementary colours; they create a sense of struggle and a lack of calm. The arrows drawn in thick lines face outwards like soldiers standing guard.

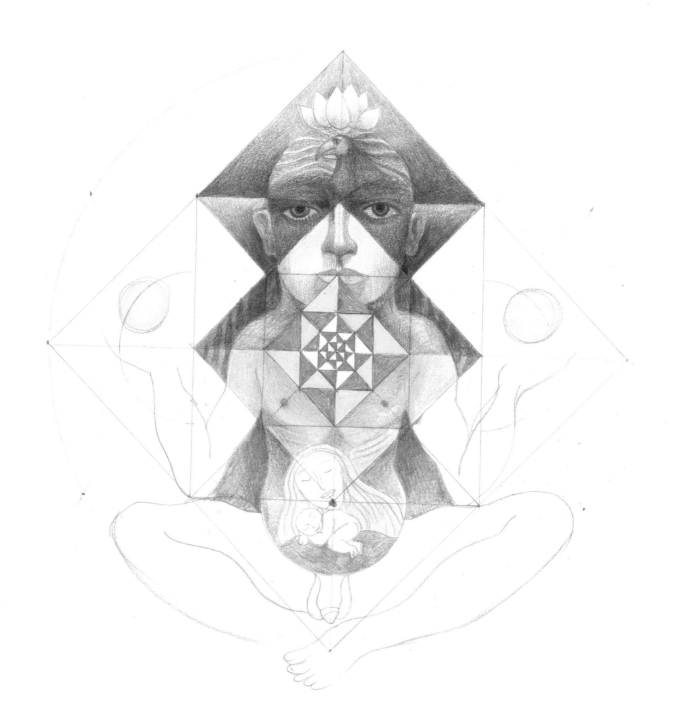

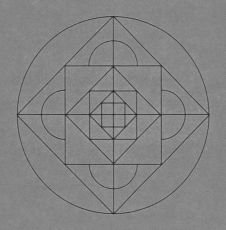

4

TIBETAN MANDALA
RETURNING HOME

How do I feel in my body?
What is my life's path and purpose in this world?
What are my internal and external worlds?

The History of the Tibetan Mandala

In times past, when people set out to explore unknown expanses, they looked for means to guide their way. The starting point was the circular horizon line. If we imagine our body as the centre point of our spatial orientation, then the body with arms outstretched sideways creates a left–right orientation. Imagine lines extending outwards from both sides of the body until they meet. Thus we can imagine the classical mandala form based on the circular horizon line and four lines that meet in the body: the centre of the circle.

The division of space into the four directions of the compass is very grounding. Devout Christians mark themselves with these four directions when they make the sign of the cross as an act that acknowledges their faith in God. When we are conscious of the four directions – above, below, right and left, or north, south, east and west – we become enveloped by a sense of presence and confidence in the world because we know where to locate ourselves, where we are going and where we are coming from.

The number four symbolizes the world, substance, materiality and, thus, our physical bodies. Many traditions believe that our body is a temple in which God dwells. However, when the soul dwells within the body, it is in a state of constriction. The material world is much more constricted than the realm of the soul; however, we enter this limited and restricted world for a purpose – to repair the soul and achieve wholeness. That is the reason we repeatedly go through the journey of life from the square, symbolizing the physical, to the circle, symbolizing divine wholeness.

The squared mandala brings us back to the boundaries of the self, to a feeling of being enveloped. It calms in times of illness and stress. Drawing within the square soothes, stabilizes and gives a feeling of security, inner quiet and healing. The squared mandala confronts us with feelings of borders and limitations. Take time to notice what feelings arise while drawing the square. It can remind us of the homes we have lived in, and what we felt in the house we grew up in. The mandala examines the distinction we make between our personal borders and the outside world. The square provides an opportunity to examine our relationship with our physical body. Do we nurture it? Do we forget about it? Do we see it only as a vehicle for the soul? We can examine how much we appreciate, honour and love our body. Lack of attention to the body's need for rest, enjoyment and proper nutrition are factors in disease and pain. Creating a squared mandala can disclose our relationship to the material world and the objects that surround us. We can observe the degree to which we hold onto objects or images that no longer serve our needs.

The Tibetan mandala creates a dialogue between the circle and the square and denotes the transition between this world and the one beyond. The four gates on the sides of the square form entrances and exits to and from the physical world and our spiritual essence.

The Tibetan Mandala and the Kalachakra (Wheel of Time) Mandala

For the Tibetan Buddhists, the mandala symbolizes a model of a perfect world and opens the gate to eternal happiness. By contemplating and creating the mandala in various materials, believers visualize the Buddha and the Buddhist path to enlightenment.

The word for mandala in Tibetan, *dkyil khor*, means the centre of the circle. One of the more famous and familiar of the many Tibetan mandalas is called Kalachakra, whose literal translation is "wheel of time". This circle symbolizes the passage from earthly life to pure, enlightened consciousness. The deity Kalachakra is one of the manifestations of Buddha. He stands in the centre of the mandala, unified with his feminine consort, Vishvamata, the universal mother. The union between them is the unification of supreme compassion and wisdom, which is the objective of all Buddhist strivings. Upon arriving at the point of unification, he undergoes purification and rebirth, forever leaving the regular life of mortals chained to the wheel of life and death, and crosses over to an eternal life of lasting happiness

According to Buddhist belief, a quick glance at the mandala is enough to awaken awareness and begin to grow in the direction of the light. The path to the absolute light is long and arduous, filled with tests and lessons. The only way to reach it is by way of the four open gateways to the four directions, which look like the letter "T". A guard sitting at each gateway meticulously examines the believers' virtue before deciding i f they should be allowed to pass through or remain outside the gate and keep working. The mandala is a schematic architectural model of a spacious, magnificent palace ascending to the heavens. The five intertwining squares create five levels or floors. Each one is a mandala in itself, representing a stage of spiritual development; the ultimate objective is to reach the point at the edge of the roof where great happiness awaits. When the student succeeds in entering the palace, 722 divinities are there to teach them all that they need to know to go on to the next stage. On each level, the student studies the subject that belongs to that level: the lowest and widest level focuses on the human body; the second level addresses speech; the third is the level of thought; the fourth investigates consciousness; the top level is the sacred space of supreme happiness.

According to the Buddhist tradition, each detail and colour in the mandala has symbolic meaning. White, found in the north, represents the element of water, and the qualities of purity, knowledge and longevity. As mentioned previously, in the Tibetan Buddhist tradition, the white north is the masculine side and is symbolized by the moon. Red, found in the south, on the mandala's left side, represents the element of fire, the life force, protection and sanctity. This is the feminine side and is represented by the sun. Yellow is found in the mandala's upper quadrant and is the west. Yellow is the colour of earth and represents the stability of the ground, humility and rebirth. Blue, found in the east, in the lower quadrant of the mandala, represents the air element, wisdom, tranquility, elation, purity and healing. Black represents the darkness. Out of the dark are created light and colour, and they create sound. Sound creates form. The significance of the colour black is the turning of bad into good. Occasionally blue and black change places. Green represents the active energy of youth, and also harmony and balance.

The palace is surrounded by six protective circles that guard and protect the mandala's purity and represent the elements composing the universe. The largest and outermost ring is the ring of wisdom. The inner rings become progressively smaller: the ring of space, the ring of spirit, the ring of fire, the ring of water and the ring of earth. The eight figures surrounding the central deity are called the eight Bodhisattvas, and are meant to signify the eight central events in the life of Buddha Shakyamuni, according to traditional teachings. Among these events are his birth, reaching enlightenment and leaving his body.

The Tibetan Sand Mandala

The mandala made from grains of coloured sand is unique to Tibetan Buddhism.

After the guru chooses the place and type of mandala, the Tibetan monks purify their bodies and souls through fasting, chanting prayers, music and meditation. Then they meticulously draw the template, according to a precise plan. They practice for seven years to achieve the level of skill required to partake in this process. The monks use simple compasses for the circles and stretched strings as rulers to make the initial drawings. Since each area of the mandala has its special sacredness, and since the diagram in general contains Buddha's guidance for reaching enlightenment, the monks are forbidden to cross the lines. Violating the mandala is so serious that it is considered analogous to breaking the monastic oath.

For several days, usually at least four monks work silently and devotedly, filling the contoured shapes with grains of sand made from finely pulverized coloured rocks. Occasionally each mandala builder has an assistant who fills the spaces previously contoured. The work is always done from the centre, the holiest point, expanding outwards. When working on the inner areas, each monk is exclusively responsible for one quarter of the mandala. As the work continues, this work pattern changes and each monk creates the forms most familiar to them according to their skills. In the past, the sand was made from pulverizing gems and semi-precious stones like coral and turquoise, but this is not the case today. Now the sand is coloured with vegetable dyes or opaque tempera and placed on the mandala using a narrow metal pipe called a chakpu, which is rubbed with another chakpu to create vibrations that cause the sand grains to drop from the tip of the chakpu. They say that the two chakpus symbolize the unity of wisdom and compassion – the essence of Buddhist practice. A chakpu with a larger opening is used for colouring the backgrounds and to create wider lines. Fine detail is made with a very narrow chakpu. The sound of the chakpus rubbing against each other is compared to emptiness, to a true understanding of the world. From out of this emptiness comes form, according to the celebrated sentence from the heart sutra: "Form is emptiness; emptiness is form. Form is no different than emptiness; emptiness is no different than form".

Some of the spaces of the mandala are filled with tiny stones of coloured gravel. Frequently the completion of the mandala is planned to occur on the night of a full moon, which represents mindfulness and awareness, characteristics which the mandala is meant to sharpen. Every so often a monk brings those working hot tea or food. Breaks are short and fixed, but the atmosphere during the whole process is tranquil and calm. Generally there is complete silence, punctuated only by the workers coordinating small, practical matters and the sounds of the chakpu funnels rubbing against each other. When the mandala is completed, the monks cover it with glass in a wood frame to protect it from harm. They are then given a short time to enjoy their handiwork.

After a number of days, during which special prayers are conducted, a ceremony is held, sealing the dedication of the mandala. A simple mandala, dedicated to the fire element and made with relatively crude lines without the use of chakpus, is created on a small platform in the centre of the main courtyard. Dung and wood shavings are placed on this mandala and burned during the ceremony. Huge trumpets are sounded from the monastery's rooftop, calling believers to assemble for the Dismantling Ceremony.

Dressed in ceremonial garb, the head of the monastery sits on an elevated divan near the burning fire. A number of monks chanting prayers sit by their side. During the long ceremony, various offerings are presented to the head of the monastery, which they throw into the fire. After the offerings, the monastery's head monk goes to the rear of the main prayer hall where the mandala is located, and those in attendance follow him. The monks sit down in their places and begin to chant. Accompanied by drums, cymbals and bells, they ask the deities to leave the mandala.

At the end of the prayers a few monks remove the glass covering and the head of the monastery approaches. He removes the deities that are manifested in the mandala in the reverse order of their construction. The head monk takes a pinch of sand in his fingertips, symbolizing the supreme qualities found within the mandala. Then, using the vajra, symbol of supreme compassion, he divides the mandala from east to west, from north to south and in diagonals. After removing the divine powers from the mandala, the monks sweep the sand from the periphery toward the centre. The areas of coloured sand and finely executed shapes that were so meticulously assembled immediately disappear. As all the colourful shades of sand combine, the sand takes on a greyish shade. Some of the sand is placed in the outstretched hands of believers. They swallow a bit and collect the rest in a small bag that they will bury near the foundation of their homes or dilute in their drinking water, a source of blessings. The rest of the sand is collected into an urn. Then a cloth is used to erase the initial sketch.

Nothing is left of the mandala. Wrapped in what looks like royal cloth, the urn is carried out of the monastery premises to the nearby river with great honour and ceremony in a colourful, festive procession. Monks playing the drums and trumpets march before the urn bearer. A last, short prayer is held at the water's edge, in which the monks ask the spirits residing within the water to receive the mandala. The monks visualize that all life in the water is blessed with abundance and that the purified waters evaporate to return as precipitation, raining down on all the creatures of the earth, cleansing the world of illusion and bringing salvation. The urn is stripped of its colourful wrappings. Then one of the monks takes the urn and pours its contents into the water. The dismantling of the mandala is a lesson in non-attachment and impermanence. According to Buddhist belief, everything in our world is temporary.

According to Buddhism, each person is, in fact, a complete mandala, a circle existing within their family circle and their circle of friends and acquaintances, with reciprocal relations between themselves and these other expanding circles of life. Humanity, like everything else in this world, has strong, inseparable ties with their surroundings. The "I" is an axis around which events revolve. The Buddhist student seeks to understand the relationship between their body and the mandala, and the relationship between the deities within the mandala and the universe. Using these insights, they are meant to return to their physical body and erect an inner temple. The uniqueness of Tibetan Buddhism is that humanity's purpose does not end with personal enlightenment and salvation, but with aiding all other sentient beings to attain enlightenment.

Tibetan Mandala Meditation

Sit in a comfortable position on a chair or pillow; make sure your spine is erect but relaxed. Imagine a ring connected to a taut string at the crown of your head pulling your spine upward, creating space, letting your lungs open wide. Close your eyes and focus on your breathing. Air enters, air exits. With each exhale, release all the tension in your body. Take seven deep breaths. Concentrate on the air that enters and exits your body. Tightly tense the muscles of your eyes, lips, shoulders, arms, hands, buttocks, abdomen, legs and feet. Then relax each body part, one after the other. Repeat this tensing and relaxing.

While breathing slowly and calmly, observe your body in your mind's eye with love and appreciation.

Place your attention on each part of your body, beginning with your feet and finishing with your head. With a heartfelt smile, acknowledge and thank each body part for its existence and its function. For example, thank your heart for pumping blood to each cell in your body without stopping for a moment. Thank your lungs for untiringly contracting and expanding, infusing your body with oxygen and releasing carbon dioxide. Thank your legs for carrying you from place to place. Thank your hands for enabling you to hold things, create drawings, etc.

After thanking your body, experience a feeling of wholeness and joy. Slowly open your eyes and move on to the drawing of the mandala.

HOW TO DRAW THE MANDALA

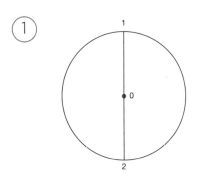

Open the compass to a radius of 9cm (3½in) and place the compass point on the centre of the page. Draw a circle around this point, and then draw a diameter halving the circle vertically (line 1–2). Make sure that line 1–2 passes through point 0 and is parallel to the edges of the paper.

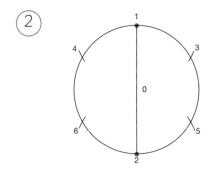

Place the point of the compass at point 1 and mark the points intersecting the circle: to the right at point 3 and to the left at point 4. Repeat this process from point 2 and mark intersection points 5 to the right and point 6 to the left.

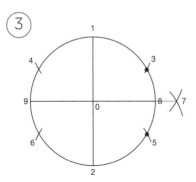

3

Place the point of the compass at points 3 and 5, and mark two small arcs opposite point 0, that intersect at point 7. Connecting points 7 and 0 with a ruler, draw the horizontal diameter of the circle, line 8–9.

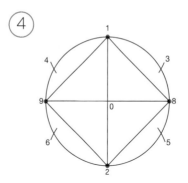

4

Create the first square by connecting points 1, 8, 2 and 9.

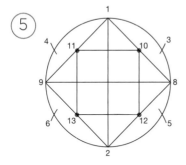

5

Place the ruler at points 3 and 4 and draw line 10–11. Then place the ruler at points 5 and 6 and draw line 12–13. Connect points 11–13 and 10–12 to create the second square.

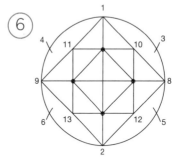

6

Create the third square by connecting the points where the lines of the second square intersect the vertical and horizontal diameter lines.

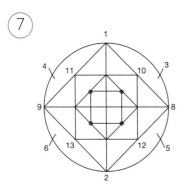

7

Draw diagonal lines between points 10–13, and 11–12. Then create the fourth square by connecting the points where the lines of the third square intersect the diagonal lines.

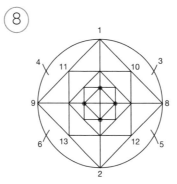

8

Create the fifth square, as per instruction 6.

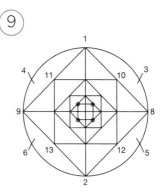

9

Create the sixth square, as per instruction 7.

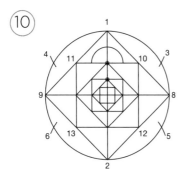

10

Place the point of the compass on the upper red dot and open the compass to a radius the distance between the two red dots. Draw a semicircle.

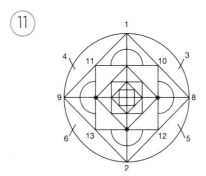

11

Draw semicircles around the three red dots, as marked.

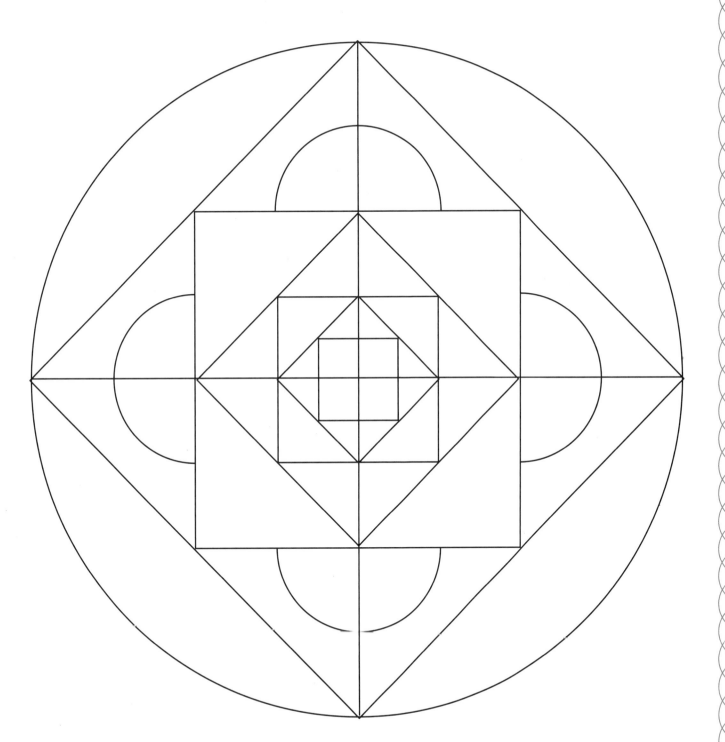

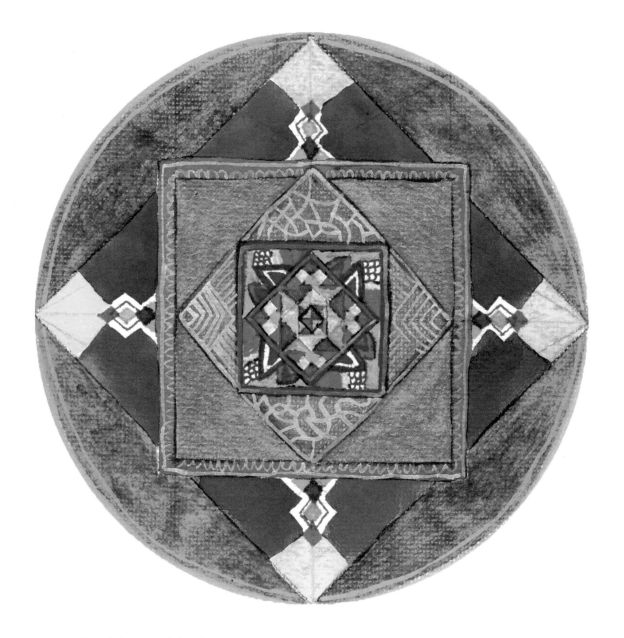

I painted this mandala while in India, sitting by the banks of the Ganges River in Rishikesh.
The square structure gave me the feeling of a home that was safe, decorative, colourful and intense,
combined with softness, simplicity and quiet – just the way I felt in India.

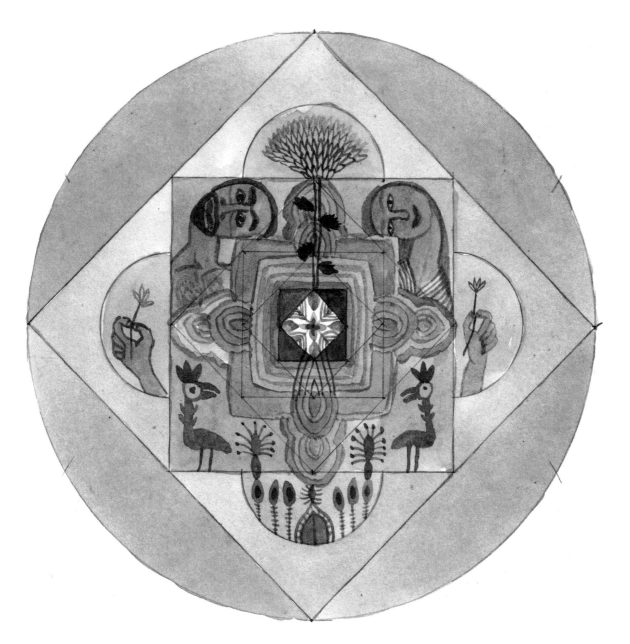

Mandala dedicated to a warm home, couplehood and family, and to the aspiration for a place where I can lay my head down and feel the comfort and quiet within myself. The warm earth colours denote protection, security and solid ground. Diluted watercolours give a feeling of transparency and tranquility.

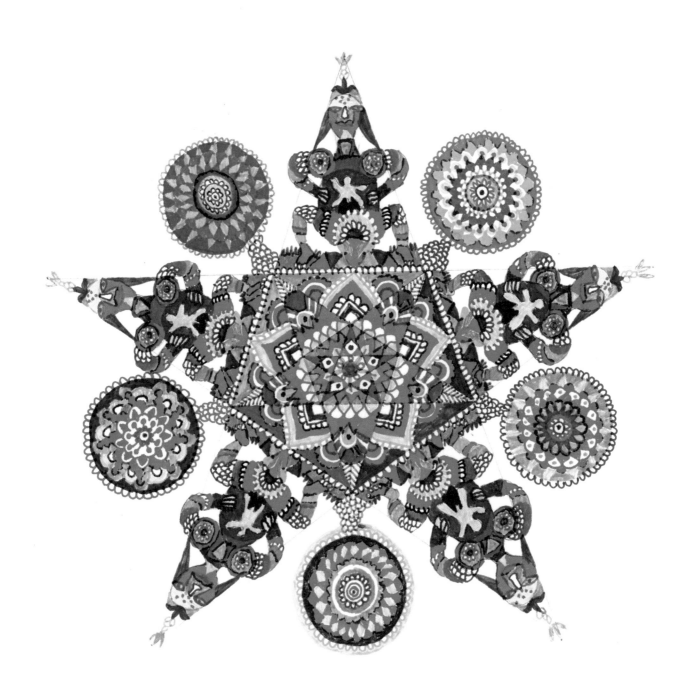

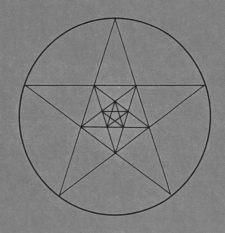

5

PENTAGONAL STAR MANDALA
THE MAGIC OF CHANGE

How do I express my abilities in the world?
How can I use the male energy that is within me?
How can I be the director of my life's script?

The History of the Pentagonal Star Mandala

The pentagonal star, or pentagram, is made from dividing a circle into five equal parts that create the pentagon. Connecting the angles of the pentagon forms five identical triangles in the form of a star. In Hebrew, this special star is called Solomon's Seal, since legend has it that this star was on the ring worn by King Solomon. King Solomon received the ring from heaven and used it to rule demons. Half of the ring was burnished brass and half was iron. King Solomon used the brass to rule the good demons and the iron to control the evil demons.

One of the reasons that the pentagram has sacred connotations is that it is one of the geometric forms in which the Golden Mean occurs naturally. The Golden Mean (or Golden Ratio) is a mathematical concept which expresses the relationship of two parts of a whole with each other and within the whole.

Represented by the Greek letter Phi, it was discovered by one of Pythagoras's students and is equal to 1.618. Its singularly pleasing visual balance is found in many forms in nature; for example, in the arrangement of branches along the stems of plants, of veins in leaves and of petals on some flowers. It is used in art, music, architecture and mathematics. Pottery makers in ancient Greece incorporated the golden mean in the ratio between the narrow mouth and the wide part of the wine-holding vessels they created. The resulting look instilled a sense of beauty and perfect form. Researchers who have studied the faces of models and movie stars famous for their beauty have found that the ratio between their facial features is the golden mean.

The pentagram is an ancient symbol from the times of the Sumerians and Babylonians. It was used by temple priests for astrological purposes, prayers and magic, and was always treated with utmost reverence. It represents the five directions: forward, back, right, left and upward. It also stands for the five elements – water, earth, fire, air and ether – as well as the five senses, the five fingers and the five knightly virtues: sincerity, friendship, purity, courtesy and compassion.

Pentagrams are found in abundance in magic papyruses and amulets from ancient times. The names generally found on these items are the Jewish names of God – Adonai, Tzvaot, Shaddai, Elohim – and the names of Jesus of Nazareth, and of Greek, Roman and Egyptian gods. They were used for protection and for taking oaths, and for talismans against malaria and other diseases.

The number five represents masculine energy that is active and has the power to change things and move them in new directions. This is highly focused energy with clear boundaries; it is energy that sharpens, hones and acts without compromise. The energy of the number five is not balanced. There is no rest or repose; it constantly acts and activates. One can imagine the energy of the five as a knight in armour fighting with a drawn, sharpened sword, showing no emotions.

The Pentagonal Star characterizes the power of the leader, particularly the ability to focus on a goal and bring it to fruition. The sense of masculine power in this symbol is seen in its frequent use in medals, sports symbols and symbols of military ranks. The masculine feeling of victory is symbolized by the star on the flags of the USA, Ethiopia, Turkey and Morocco. The Seal of Solomon is perceived as a symbol of magic in Japanese culture, and also appears as the symbol of secret societies associated with magic and spells.

The pentagram was one of the main symbols of the city of Jerusalem between the years 300 and 150 BC. The first Christians used it as a symbol of Jesus's five crucifixion wounds. The pentagram appears in Jewish writings in the 9th century AD. In many texts it can be found instead of the Star of David, and vice versa. Apparently the Star of David and the pentagram developed concurrently as symbols in Jewish history and, for a time, they were used interchangeably. Hexagrams and pentagrams can be found carved in ancient synagogues, occasionally even in place of the mezuzah, which testifies to their use as a protective talisman.

Solomon's Seal represents the perfect body. The upper triangle represents the head, and the four other triangles are the two arms and two legs. However, if we turn it upside down, we have the horned devil. Satan represents the power of magic and its ability to change shape and substance. The two upper triangles, or goat's horns, symbolize pride and strength. The two side triangles, or goat's ears, signify the two sides of every coin or the two sides to each story. The forehead of the goat is the third side of the coin: what we think about the story we heard. The lower triangle represents the mouth of the goat, symbolizing earthly speech and all earthly things. We can use the power of Solomon's Seal to heal pain that is concentrated in one spot; for example, knee pain or lower back pain. Using our imagination, we focus the pentagonal symbol on the injured area and draw a pentagram mandala to help release the pain. This mandala is excellent for opening areas that are blocked energetically. The pentagonal mandala stimulates our masculine energy: to take action, to be active, to set things in motion, to focus and clarify thoughts and to make decisions. Remember that the symbol of the five-pointed star holds intense energy with the power to change and influence, thus it should be used in a balanced and moderate way. Occasionally this mandala awakens strong reactions in the person drawing it. Some people may feel restless or insecure. Should such feelings occur, let them rise into your consciousness, remembering that everything that comes up during the mandala drawing comes to heal us. Particularly pay attention to the way you feel about the sharp points of the star. Recall that the star symbolizes masculine energy, particularly its sharp angles, reminiscent of knights charging with drawn swords toward a sacred goal. Notice while drawing if you curve or blunt the points or ignore the decisive, clear presence of the format. This could point to your not being ready to act openly and decisively, preferring to act privately or in secret.

Pentagonal Star Meditation

Sit in a comfortable position on a chair or pillow; make sure your spine is erect but relaxed. Imagine a ring connected to a taut string at the crown of your head pulling your spine upward, creating space, letting your lungs open wide. Close your eyes and focus on your breathing. Air enters, air exits. With each exhale, release all the tension in your body. Take seven deep breaths. Concentrate on the air that enters and exits your body. Tightly tense the muscles of your eyes, lips, shoulders, arms, hands, buttocks, abdomen, legs and feet. Then relax each body part, one after the other. Repeat this tensing and relaxing.

While breathing quietly and deeply, look at your body in your mind's eye. Scan the different parts from head to toe and find the areas where the energy is blocked. If you feel tightness or pain, place your hands, one over the other, on this spot. Breathe into the blocked area, using deep, regular breaths that will help to release the blockages.

Slowly, return to the feeling of here and now and open your eyes. Move on to the drawing of the mandala.

HOW TO DRAW THE MANDALA

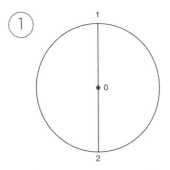

Open the compass to a radius of 9cm (3½in) and place the compass point on the centre of the page. Draw a circle around this point. Then draw a vertical diameter, line 1–2. Make sure that line 1–2 passes thought point 0 and is parallel to the paper's edges.

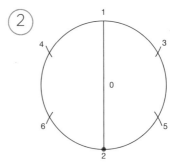

Place the point of the compass at point 1 and mark the points intersecting the circle: points 3 to the right and 4 to the left. Repeat this process from point 2, marking intersecting points 5 to the right and 6 to the left.

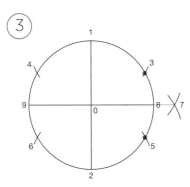

3

Placing the point of the compass at points 3 and 5, mark small arcs opposite point 0 and mark their intersection point, point 7. Connect points 7 and 0 with a ruler and draw the horizontal diameter of the circle, marking points 8 and 9 where the horizontal diameter intersects the circle.

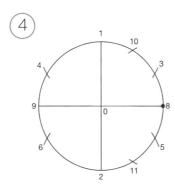

4

Place the point of the compass at point 8 and mark the intersecting points on the circle: 10 above and 11 below.

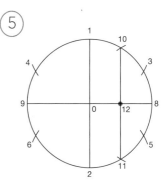

5

Connect points 10 and 11 using a ruler and mark point 12 where line 10–11 intersects the horizontal diameter.

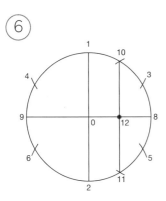

6

Place the point of the compass on point 12 and open the compass until it reaches point 1.

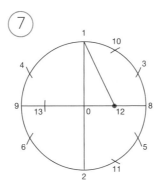

7

With the compass point still at point 12, mark the intersection with line 8–9 as point 13.

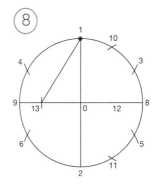

8

Place the point of the compass at point 1 and open the compass until it reaches point 13.

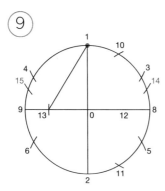

9

With the compass point still at point 1, mark the points of intersection with the circle: point 14 to the right and point 15 to the left.

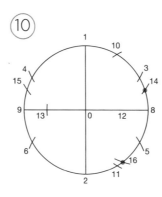

10

Place the point of the compass at point 14 and mark the point intersecting the circle at point 16.

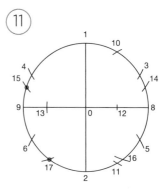

11

Place the compass point at point 15 and mark the point intersecting the circle at point 17.

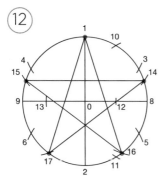

12

To draw the star, connect points 1, 17, 14, 15, 16 as in the illustration.

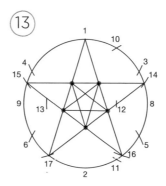

13

Draw the inner star by connecting the intersection points on the star as in the illustration.

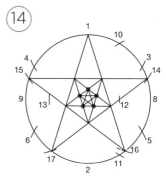

14

Draw another inner star by connecting the intersection points on the star as in the illustration.

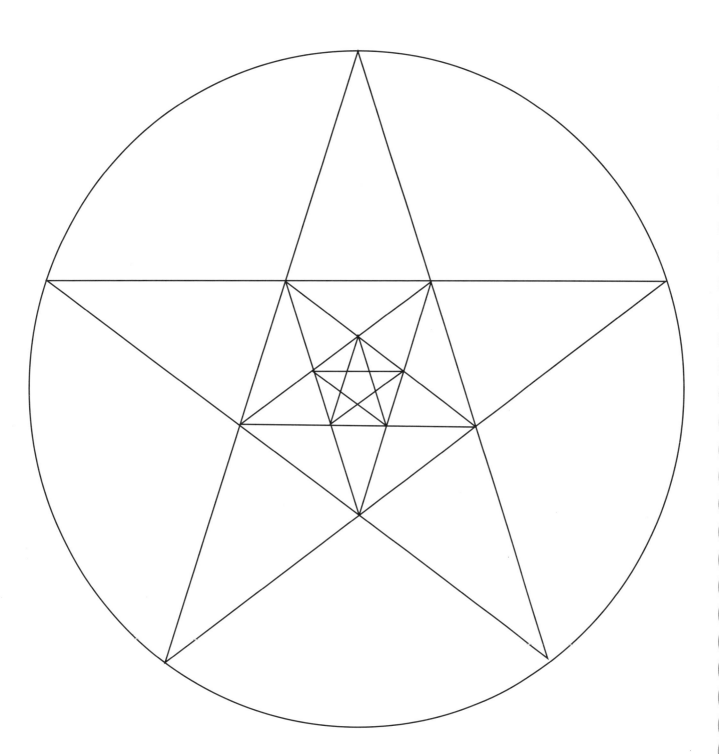

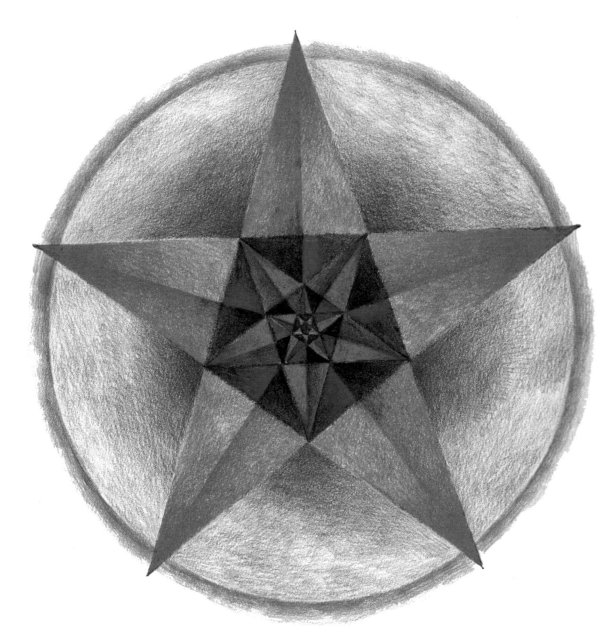

I drew this mandala to try to communicate with the masculine parts within me. I wanted to experience the feeling of control that characterizes a man full of confidence and sure of himself, who lets no obstacle stand in his way. Drawing in pencil makes it easier to create a sense of three dimensions. The muted, restrained colours enhance the feeling of power conveyed by the five-pointed star.

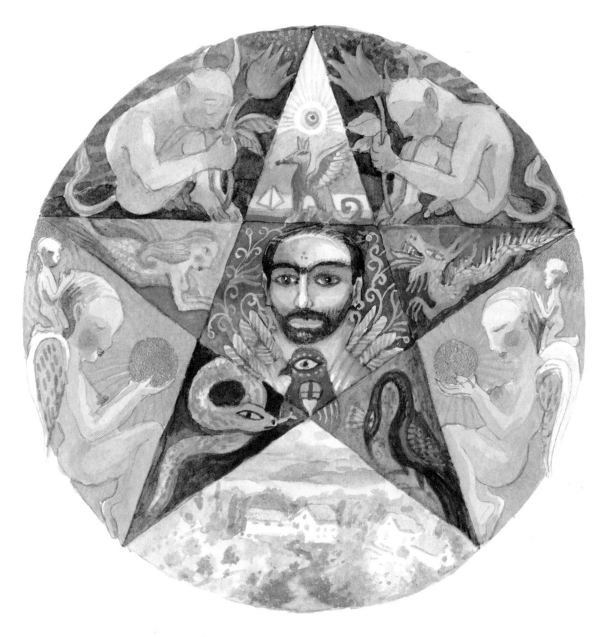

The five-pointed star always touches me in hidden, unfamiliar places, and opens within me a Pandora's Box where dark demons hide. I felt that the demons and the angels had come out to talk to each other. The angels are holding golden balls of light and the demons have withdrawn into themselves. The house looks pastoral from the outside but does not reveal the demons hiding inside.

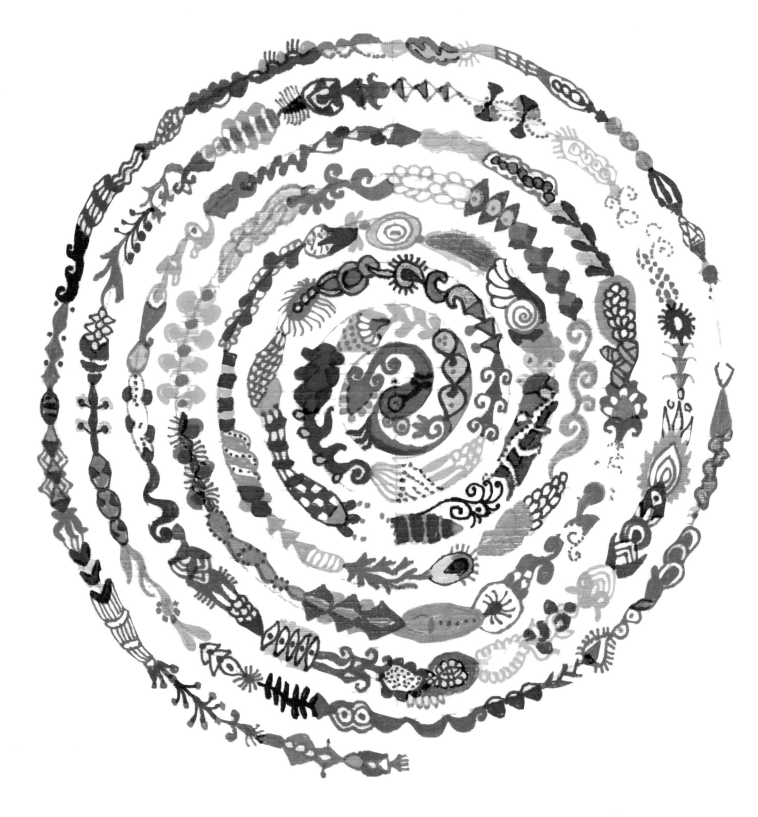

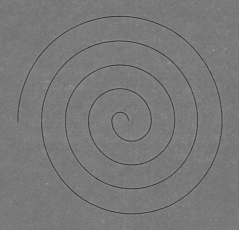

6

SPIRAL MANDALA
THE PATH OF LIFE

How does my life's path look?
What is the inner voice that guides me on my path?
How can I shed the old so that I can be open to the new?

The History of the Spiral Mandala

The spiral is a curved line that emanates from a central point and forms ever-widening circles as it moves away from and revolves around its point of origin. An excellent example of the spiral form in nature can be seen in conches, which are formed by rotating around a fixed axis. The nautilus conch shell has a logarithmic spiral structure that grows according to the golden mean. The spiral is found in the horns, nails and teeth of animals, and among many plants. It is an ancient symbol that is found in Stone Age drawings and in ancient burial sites all over the world.

In ancient China the spiral symbol represented the sun being reborn every morning. It signifies life energy and the eternal present. Its shape is three-dimensional and it can expand infinitely. It illustrates the cyclical movement in which we live. At any given moment we are in a new place, from which we see the world from a broader perspective.

At each moment in time, we have the possibility to be reborn and to see the world and ourselves in a different way. If we can connect to the here and now, the path will open before us. In the spiral drawing, as in life, no point repeats itself. Our progress is like a path which unfolds anew at every moment. The spiral is in constant motion, a motion which is energetic and continually changing. "No man ever steps into the same river twice," said the Greek philosopher Heraclitus. While painting the spiral we re-experience how we make our way in the world.

In Indian culture, the kundalini (energy that lies dormant at the base of the spine) can wind like a spiral snake up to the crown chakra at the top of the head once it is activated. The meaning of the word "kundalini" in Sanskrit is "curled like a spiral", wound like a spring or coil. This latent spiritual energy which dwells within us is like a taut and coiled spring ready to be released and shoot opward. In its dormant state it is in the root chakra. When we are ready to begin a spiritual process, the right situation is created, the kundalini energy awakens within us and the spring is released. The energy rises up the spinal column, opening and activating the chakras' energy centres, from the first chakra (at the base of the spine) to the seventh chakra (at the crown of the head), and connects to the essence of Oneness, enabling us to experience supreme bliss, to experience who we really are.

The cosmic energy within us maintains all the processes of life, creation, preservation, being, the energy of love and intelligence, which is in the cosmos and in ourselves. This energy has different names in different cultures. In ancient Chinese writings it is called Chi, and from here comes the name Tai Chi; in Japan it is called Ki, and from this source is the name Aikido. Both are ancient healing martial arts.

Kundalini energy maintains all the life processes in the physical body: consciousness, thinking, breathing, metabolism, blood flow, heart beats, sexuality, fertility, illness and healing. It is awake and active in all living creatures at different levels and intensity according to their inner qualities, and embodies health, creativity and ability for physical and mental renewal. This is the spiritual energy that connects us to wholeness, to the inner Self, and unites us with the cosmic whole.

Drawing the spiral mandala allows us to experience a feeling of openness and release and increases the flow of energy in the body, which is vital for health. The spiral opens blocked places and infuses new blood full of vitality and vigor. Through the spiral we can see our unique life's path and the different circles that comprise it. The spiral is associated with the right side of the brain, the intuitive side, letting the left side – which, in Western culture, is the one in charge, the logical one with clear goals that never stops working for a moment – to rest a bit.

It is preferable to draw the spiral from the centre, in a clockwise direction, in harmony with the earth's movement. The spiral comes to teach us to open and receive the gifts that life brings to us. To do so, we must let go of all that is old, all the beliefs, the objects and the things that we hold onto from lack of faith. This is the time to look at the choices we make in our lives; we need to listen to an inner voice to know the right time to act and the right time to rest and gather strength. Thus we will enable ourselves to live according to the rhythm that suits us.

We begin our mandala drawing with a short warm-up spiral. Take a piece of chalk or oil crayons and rapidly doodle spirals on a large sheet of paper. Try drawing first with your right hand and then with your left hand, and then with both hands at the same time. Change the direction, drawing the spiral from the inside out and then from the outside in; draw clockwise and then counterclockwise. The purpose of this exercise is to get the energy moving. This is an especially good exercise to do when our energy is lower than usual.

The mandala spiral can be drawn according to a precise template (see directions below) or freehand, according to your inner rhythm.

Spiral Mandala Meditation

Sit in a comfortable position on a chair or pillow; make sure your spine is erect but relaxed. Imagine a ring connected to a taut string at the crown of your head pulling your spine upward, creating space, letting your lungs open wide. Close your eyes and focus on your breathing. Air enters, air exits. With each exhale, release all the tension in your body. Take seven deep breaths. Concentrate on the air that enters and exits your body. Tightly tense the muscles of your eyes, lips, shoulders, arms, hands, buttocks, abdomen, legs and feet. Then relax each body part, one after the other. Repeat this tensing and relaxing. While breathing quietly and deeply, visualize your life as a spiral expanding in ever-widening circles from the moment of your birth, represented by the bindu point. See the road that you travelled during the first seven years of your life. Then look at the next seven years. What was your life's path then? Continue the visualization in seven-year increments until you reach the present. Give thanks with a smile for all your choices; in each period there were turning points that were signposts for change, growth and development. This is your unique path with its ups and downs, and moments of joy and crises from which you have grown. Give thanks for all the gifts that have flowed to you, and for the support and love you have received from near and far. See how life has channelled you toward your life's purpose.

After you reach the here and now of your life's path, take a few more quiet breaths. Slowly open your eyes and begin to draw the mandala.

HOW TO DRAW THE MANDALA

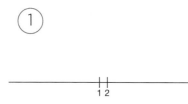

Draw a horizontal line in the middle of the page and mark it with two points that are 3mm (¹⁄₁₀in) apart (points 1 and 2).

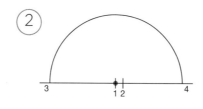

Open the compass to a radius of 9cm (3½in). Place the compass point at point 1 and draw a semicircle above the line (points 3 and 4).

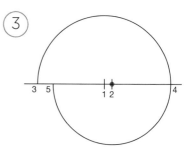

Decrease the compass radius to the length of line 2–4, place the compass point at point 2 and draw a semicircle below the line (points 4 and 5).

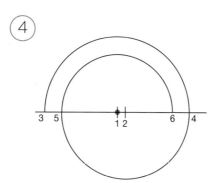

Decrease the radius to the length of line 1–5, place the point of the compass at point 1 and draw a semicircle above the line (points 5 and 6).

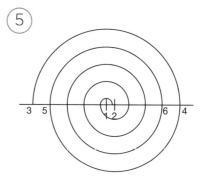

Continue in this way, alternating between placing the compass point at points 1 and 2. Don't forget to decrease the radius appropriately at each stage.

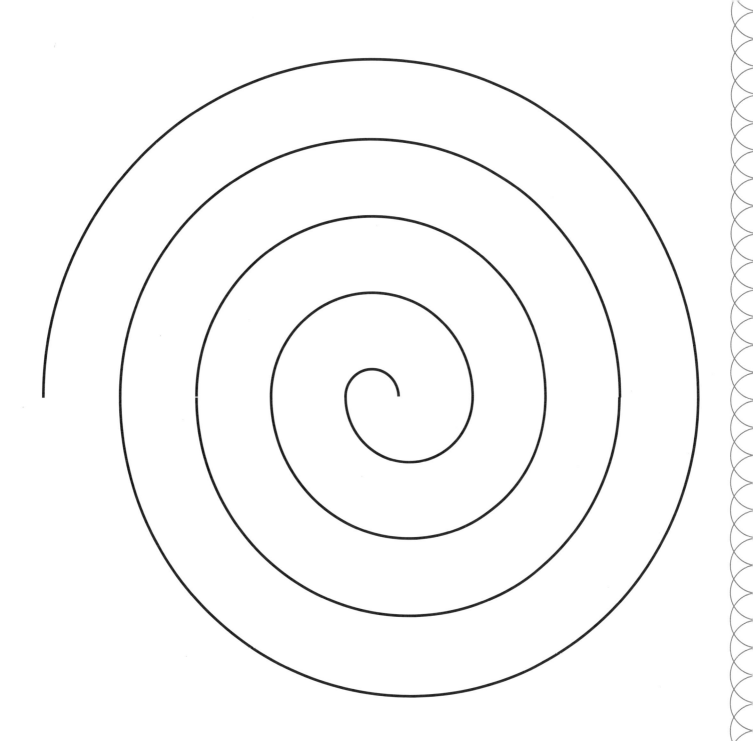

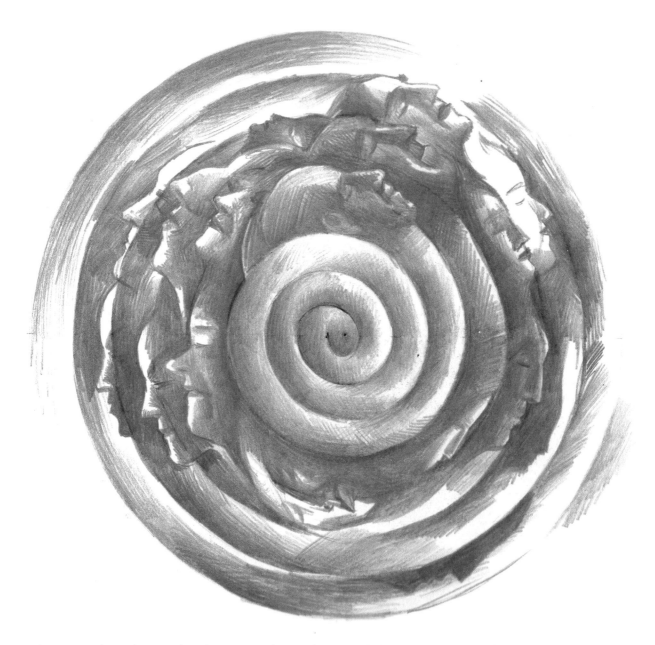

I began to draw this spiral as the image of an underground channel. As I drew, I felt drawn back in time. I saw faces of men and women of different ages. Perhaps I know them from other lifetimes. The red connects me to ancient roots, longing for the simplicity of tribal living.

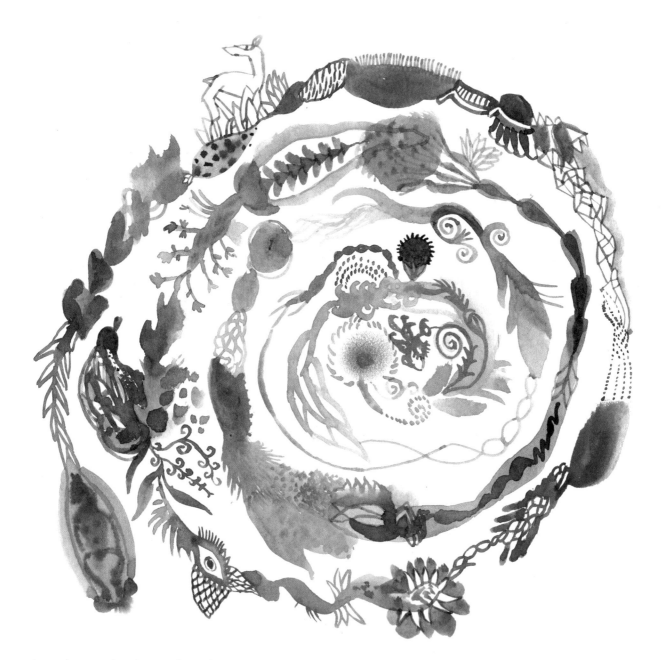

I drew this spiral without a formal template. As one shape developed into the next, I experienced what it is to live without knowing exactly where the road is leading. I enjoyed surprising myself with colours, shapes and new images that appeared to me. I was able to give myself up to the images and let them flow without control.

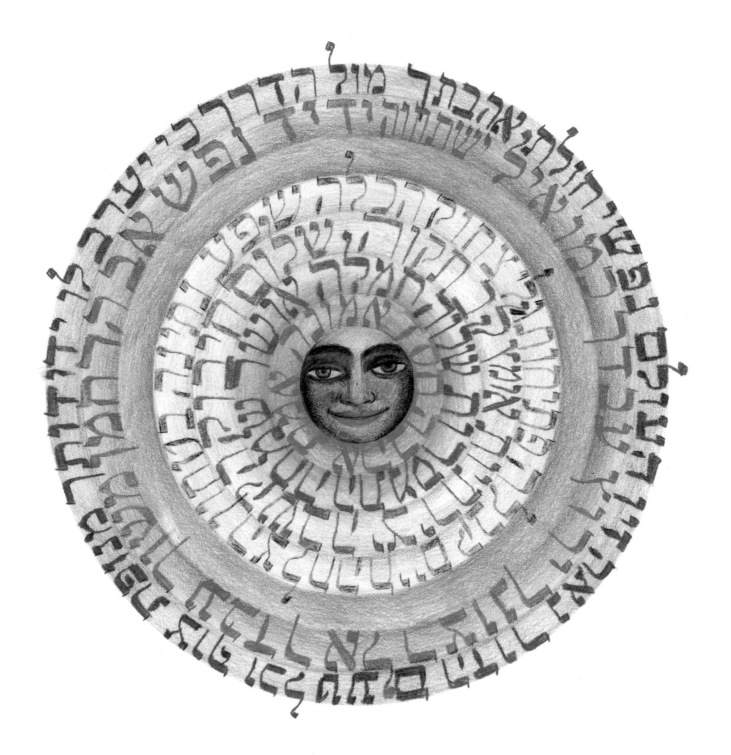

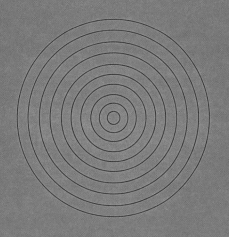

7
MANDALA OF WORDS
BLESSINGS AND PRAYERS

Do words have the power to change reality?
Do I sense the divine presence within me?
Whom do I wish to bless?

The History of the Mandala of Words

A devout Jew awakens in the morning and blesses God for returning their soul. A Hindu monk awakens at sunrise, dips themselves in the holy waters of the Ganges and blesses the rising sun. Muslims say their morning prayers, calling, "God is great", and prostrate themselves in the direction of the holy city of Mecca. Religions throughout the world use words as a basic means to communicate with God. Blessings and prayers serve to remind us of the presence of God and give us the opportunity to give thanks for the gifts that we receive.

Moses turned to God, requesting that he forgive his sister Miriam and heal her leprosy. "And Moses cried unto the Lord, saying, 'Heal her now, O God, I beseech Thee.'" (Leviticus 12:13) Jesus composed the Lord's Prayer and passed it on to his pupils: "Our Father who art in heaven, hallowed be thy name. Thy kingdom come, Thy will be done on earth as it is in heaven. Give us this day our daily bread, and forgive us our trespasses as we forgive those who trespass against us, and lead us not into temptation, but deliver us from evil. Amen."

We pray in various situations: at births and deaths, in hours of distress, in moments of exhilaration from nature, in gratitude and in love. Some people pray every day, and some people pray at special moments, prayers that spontaneously arise.

In this lesson we look at a different, very rich group of mandalas in which the written word gives the mandala its special quality. In our day-to-day life, writing is often an automatic activity. We are used to writing letters, articles, papers, notes, lists, etc. Writing within a mandala affords an opportunity to relate to writing in a more intentional and meaningful way. Throughout history, temple priests wrote sacred words and special requests within circular forms. They believed that the words would reach their destination faster and would be answered more quickly than if they were written in an ordinary way. In Japan and India, for example, yantras (mystical diagrams) with words and numbers are part of religious ceremonies. Believers write the sacred sounds called mantras on the yantras as a means of coming closer to pure happiness.

Calligraphy is a way of life in China and Japan. The Japanese word for calligraphy, shodo, means the writing path, with the emphasis on path and not on the result. Calligraphy is a daily activity. In Zen philosophy in Japan, calligraphy has great significance. The letter is written meticulously, keeping in mind its special rhythm and movement that serves as a mirror of the writer's spiritual development. Complete devotion is required from the pupil and the teacher. In the South Korean movie, *Spring, Summer, Fall, Winter and Spring*, the young man who killed his lover is told by the master that he must carve the calligraphy of the heart sutra, using a cat's tail, for a period of 24 hours. In this scene, the audience witnesses the great change that comes over the young man, from rage, fear and confusion to calm, understanding and wholeness.

Calligraphy, from the Greek, meaning "beautiful writing", is an integral part of Islamic art. In Judaism, calligraphy also has a significant place. The Torah scroll is always handwritten in letters drawn by a Sofer STaM – a trained scribe for Hebrew religious texts – who writes with a feather and ink. Judaism does not permit sculpture or figurative drawings of humans, based on the Third Commandment ("Thou shalt not make unto thee any graven image, or any likeness [of anything] that [is] in heaven above, or that [is] on the earth beneath, or that [is] in the water under the earth"). The focus is on the abstract and eternal and not on earthly forms.

This prohibition also exists in Islam and, as a result, a complete school of calligraphy, based on writing the names of God within circular forms, developed. It is said that Muhammad, seeing his wife embroidering a pillow, rebuked her and said, "Angels do not enter a home with images, and the makers of images will be punished on Judgement Day". The invention of Arabic script is attributed to Allah, and the use of the pen is considered an important skill that Allah gave to humanity. Thus the calligrapher's position was higher than other artists.

In Judaism we can find many examples of text writing within symbolic structures; for example, the seven-branched Menorah (candelabra). An interesting example can be seen in the handwork of Abraham Abulafia, the Spanish Kabbalist, who is known, among other things, for searching for the location of Sambation River and the Ten Lost Tribes. Abulafia arranged Kabbalistic texts in circular forms and called them "Life in the next world – circles". The circles represent the oneness of God. The explicit name of God is placed within the letter aleph.

We can relate to the words within a mandala as a power that creates reality. We can change reality by the power of thought, prayer and intention. The mandala gives validity to the heart's prayer. The lettering possibilities are many. When creating a mandala, you can use letters designed in different sizes, shapes and colours. You can choose to enlarge only one particular letter; you can write using a pen, pencil, feather, fountain pen or brush. Freehand writing of letters with a brush makes it possible to express thoughts and feelings graphically through words. You can change the significance of a word by changing its size, shape or colour.

There are many different styles of letters to choose from. We can examine what types of letters we used to write the words we chose for the mandala. Each type of letter has a meaning and a message. There are free-flowing letters, traditional decorative letters or more modern letters, sharp and square. We can highlight some of the words or certain letters within the words, thereby calling special attention to them. Why did we choose to place certain words in the centre of the mandala and others in the periphery? The act of writing the words brings hidden levels of understanding. We can also decide to change words or letters in the text as we work. It's possible to add colours, shapes, backgrounds and images within the mandala.

Consider using calligraphy when writing texts inside a mandala. There are many alphabets to choose from, and also special pens. Of course, you can add colourful embellishments to the letters. Use your imagination!

Word Meditation Mandala

Sit in a comfortable position on a chair or pillow; make sure your spine is erect but relaxed. Imagine a ring connected to a taut string at the crown of your head pulling your spine upward, creating space, letting your lungs open wide. Close your eyes and focus on your breathing. Air enters, air exits. With each exhale, release all the tension in your body. Take seven deep breaths. Concentrate on the air that enters and exits your body. Tightly tense the muscles of your eyes, lips, shoulders, arms, hands, buttocks, abdomen, legs and feet. Then relax each body part, one after the other. Repeat this tensing and relaxing.

While breathing deeply and quietly, imagine that you are leaving your house, walking on a path that leads you into a dense forest. The path winds between the trees, leading you to the home of the wise man. You knock on the door and, after a short wait, the wise man opens the door to his home. You enter, sit opposite him and ask him to write a blessing for you. The wise man writes the blessing and places it in your hand for you to read. After looking at it carefully, you collect the parchment, thank the wise man and bid him goodbye. You return on the same path, winding between the trees of the forest, until you reach home. Slowly open your eyes and return to the feeling of here and now. Move on to the drawing of your mandala of blessing.

HOW TO DRAW THE MANDALA

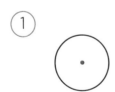

Open the compass to a radius of 1.5cm (½in) and place the compass point on the centre of the page. draw a circle around this point.

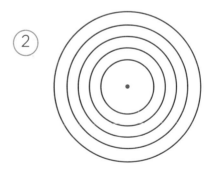

Draw increasingly bigger circles by adding 0.5cm (²/₁₀in) to the radius of each new circle.

Possible Words to Add to Your Mandala

- Choose a sentence with meaning for you from an inspiring source – for example, the Book of Psalms – and write it in the mandala.

- Dedicate this mandala of blessing to yourself or to another person.

- Listen for words that spontaneously arise from within and write them in the mandala.

- Write your name or the names of those close to you inside the mandala in different shapes, sizes and colours.

- Write an inspirational poem from a favourite poet in the mandala.

- Write a text that has significance for you in the mandala.

- Choose a word of blessing – for example, love – and write it in different ways within the mandala.

- Intuitive writing – write anything that comes to mind inside the mandala.

- Write a free text, or sounds without meaning. Use words as shapes without relating to their meaning.

- Use cards that are meant to enhance awareness/ personal understanding. Choose one card and copy its text inside the mandala.

- Choose some words, write them down next to the mandala and write a story or tale inspired by them. For example, what story can you write using the following words: hat, mushroom, diamond, frog and clown?

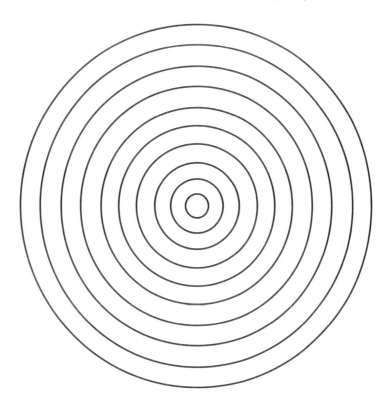

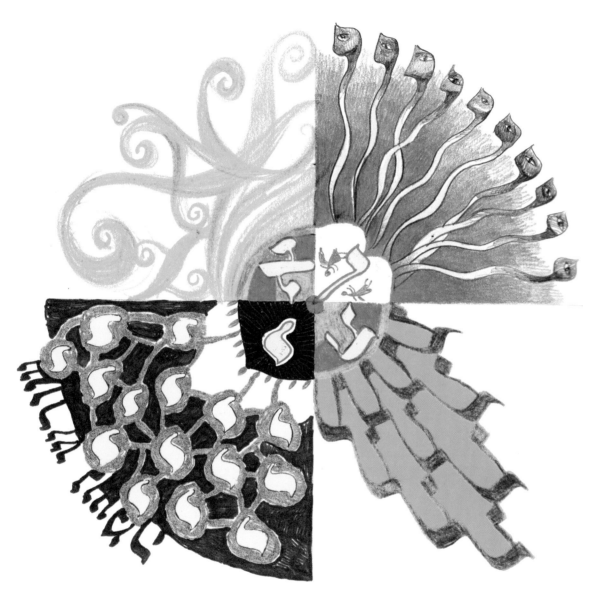

I divided the circle into quarters and wrote the letters of my name, Eitan (איתן), one opposite the other. This unusual arrangement allowed me to relate to my name from a new and surprising perspective. Aleph (א) opposite Taf (ת) – the first and last letters of the Hebrew alphabet – symbolized for me the completion of a process, with the beginning opposite the end. Aleph was innocence, filled with joy like a young boy. Taf looked like a high, mature mountain, a repository of experience and knowledge. Yod (י) looked like the root of the soul, longing for Being, the bindu. Nun (ן) was long and connected to the ground; I saw many figures in it that make up the soul.

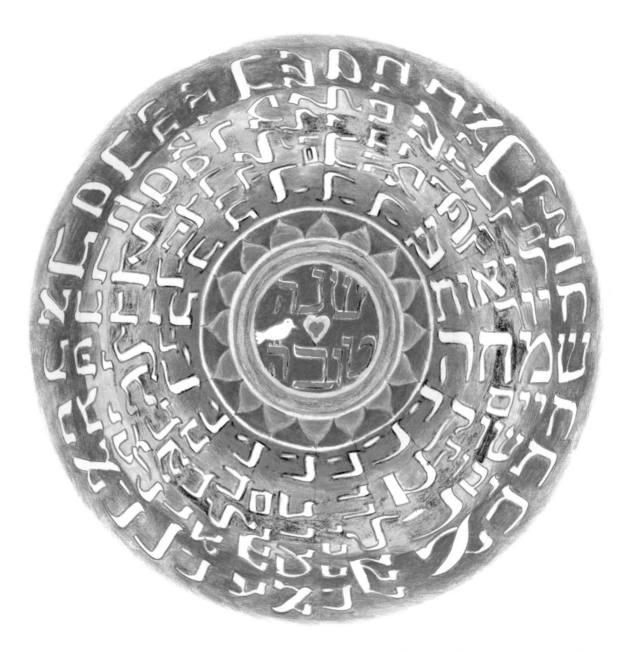

I drew this mandala to send to friends as a New Year's greeting card. First I wrote the words.
Then I coloured the background in rainbow colours to symbolize freedom, hope and openness.

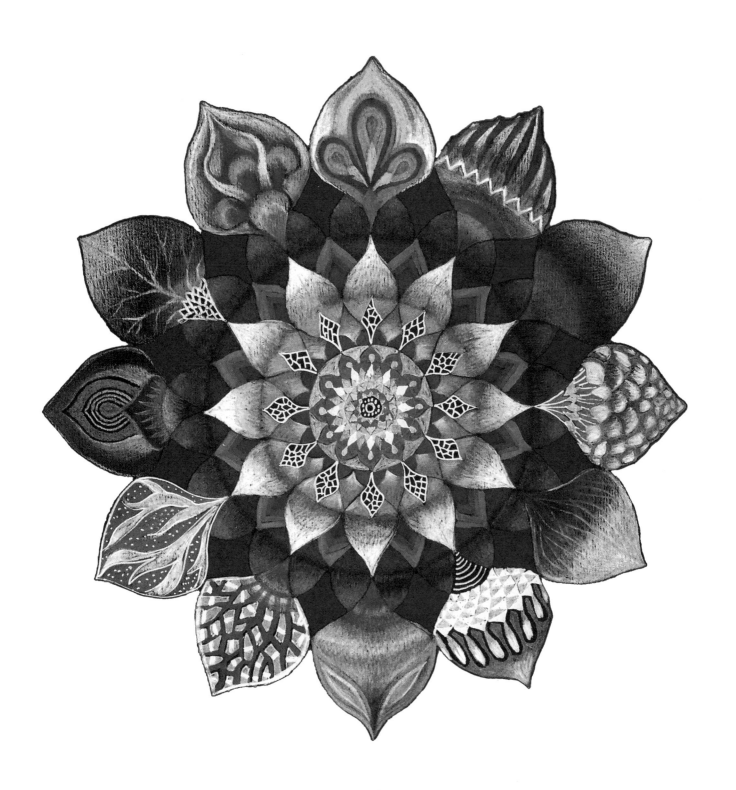

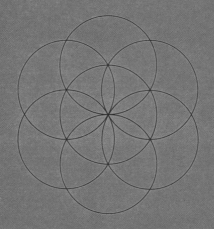

8
GROUP MANDALA
BETWEEN SACRED AND SECULAR

How to create together, in harmony?
Do I trust others?
What is my place in the group?

The History of the Group Mandala

The circle symbolizes our closest relationships. We meet our circles of friends or family at meals, during holidays or sitting around a campfire. At the beginning of civilization, our ancestors warmed themselves around a fire and came up with the revolutionary idea that sounds and voices could become a means of communication.

More than any other shape, the circle represents the feeling of a common fate, solidarity and mutual responsibility. When we sit in a circle, we see each other. A wide variety of mandalas can be made together by a family, with friends or with kids. They encourage closeness and intimacy. At the opening of the exhibition "Mandala Way" at the Wilfrid Museum at Kibbutz HaZorea, I invited Jewish and Arab artists to work together to create a colourful sand mandala. When the mandala was completed, we felt closer to each other. It would be wonderful if we were able to hold more encounters like this one between conflicting sectors – Arabs and Jews, religious and secular – in which a joint creative activity serves to bridge the gap, dispel suspicions and foster familiarity, love and acceptance.

The circle creates connection and equality among people. Many linguistic expressions include the word "circle": family circle, circle of friends, support circles, etc. We have created circles for cooperating and connecting: discussion circles, learning circles, joint meals and religious ceremonies. Almost all tribal ceremonies are done in prayer and dance circles. Creating in a circle invites acknowledgement, connection, openness, cooperation and love. The Tibetan mandala, for example, is created as a cooperative effort among monks. By creating together, they increase each other's energy and reach higher levels of spirituality. The most recommended template for a cooperative, group mandala is the Seed of Life, a simple form in which everyone can find their own personal meaning.

Group Mandala Meditation

Sit together in a circle, light a candle and play soft music. Find a comfortable position, preferably sitting on a chair or pillow, making sure your spine is erect. Imagine a ring connected to a taut string at the crown of your head pulling your spine opward, letting your lungs open wide. Close your eyes and focus on your breathing. Take seven deep breaths. If thoughts enter your mind, let them appear and gently release them. Concentrate on the air that enters and exits your body. Tightly tense the muscles of your eyes, lips, shoulders, arms, hands, buttocks, abdomen, legs and feet. Then relax each body part, one after the other. Repeat this tensing and relaxing.

Reach out and hold hands with whoever is sitting on either side of you. Your right hand gives energy, so it should be above your neighbour's left hand. Your left hand receives energy and should be under their right hand. Imagine that everyone in the circle is passing energy around the circle. Feel the shared frequency that the group transmits. Then chant the sound "Om" as a mantra together seven times. Om is a sacred Sanskrit syllable considered to have the frequency of the creation of the earth. Uttering this syllable connects us to the frequency of cooperation and empowerment. Slowly open your eyes and return to the feeling of here and now, and begin to make the group mandala.

HOW TO DRAW

1. Group Mandala on the Beach

A mandala on the beach is a surprising, unexpected sight that awakens joy, smiles and admiration from all who see it. It's so simple and so enjoyable. This kind of mandala is especially fun for kids. Add bags of coloured sand to the beach toys and enjoy a new summer beach activity. (It is important to remember that industrial pigments are not suitable for children. On page 139, you'll find a description for preparing a sand box and coloured sand suitable for children's use.)

2. A Housewarming Mandala

Holding a mandala ceremony for a new house will bless it with abundance and love, and will connect the family to their new home. First prepare seeds of varied colours: orange lentils, green mush beans, white rice, yellow corn, red beans, etc. Then add coloured spices like paprika, turmeric, cinnamon, salt and pepper.

Sit on the floor in a circle, close your eyes and breathe deeply. Choose a bindu point in a crack between the floor tiles and draw the Seed of Life pattern with a compass. Play soft music, and light some candles to create the proper ambience. Then begin to work on the mandala, using the colourful foods and spices. Between you, create a sense of non-verbal harmony. You may feel like one creature with many arms; as each arm arranges the seeds in a different area of the mandala, it will grow effortlessly of its own accord.

Once you have a completed mandala, each participant is invited to say a blessing to the homeowners, inspired by the mandala.

3. A Cooperative Mandala

Divide everyone into groups of four and provide them with a variety of drawing materials. In the centre of the table, put a large 50×50cm (20×20in) piece of cardboard with the Seed of Life template drawn on it and instruct everyone to create a mandala by working together. Every fifteen minutes, sound a gong to indicate that the participants should move in a clockwise direction to the next seat on the table.

The results are always surprising. The mandala serves as a mirror for the participants to examine themselves and the group's dynamics. Did they act freely? Who assumed the initiative and who took on leadership roles? Generally this kind of mandala is very colourful, interesting and happy, but also confusing and chaotic. It is a good opportunity to engage in a discussion of each person's role, the advantages and disadvantages of strong leadership as opposed to a lack of leadership or what makes for a harmonious group experience.

4. Leave-Taking Mandala

Each participant is asked to draw the mandala template of their choice on their paper, with their name and contact information on the back. After 15 minutes working on the mandala, the paper is passed clockwise. Every ten minutes, the mandala is passed on again until it returns to its original owner, completed and with the contact information of everyone on the back. A sharing circle is formed, and everyone discusses their experience: their ability to freely express themselves and to draw differently in another's mandala.

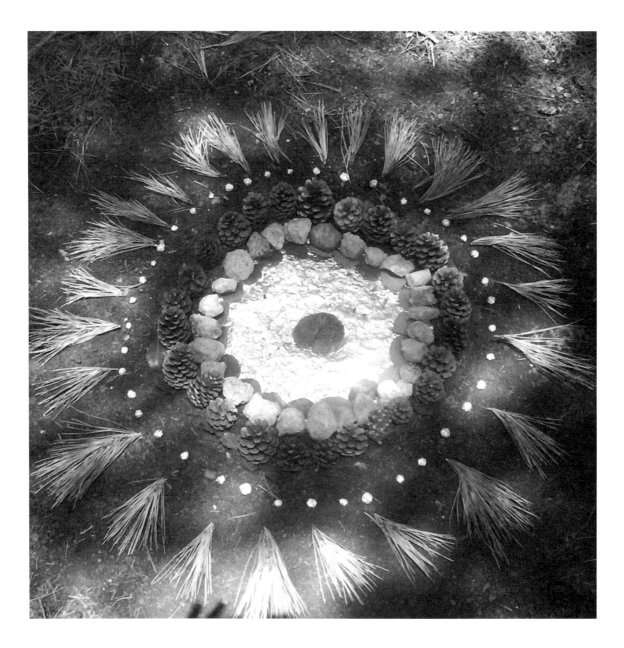

My friend Vered and her son Hillel created this mandala during an outing of families in the Ben Shemen forest. Each family was given a bag to use to collect materials from the forest. Then they chose a special place and created a mandala from the collected materials. At the end of the creative process, we visited all the mandalas and each family presented their mandala to the group.

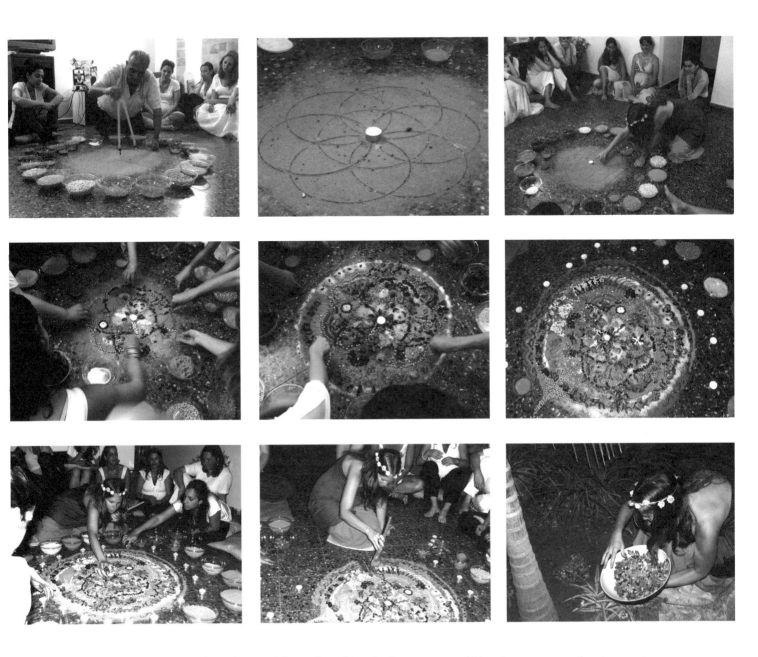

A number of days before the wedding of my friend Hila, a group of friends came together to create a mandala of blessings. We used various seeds to symbolize fertility and growth. Gaining inspiration from the finished mandala, each friend blessed Hila. Then Hila collected all the seeds from the mandala and placed them in the ground in her garden.

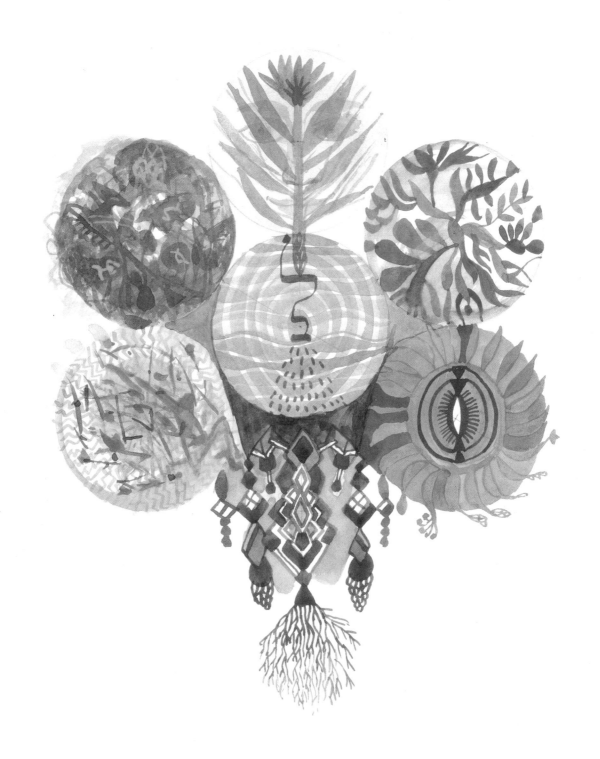

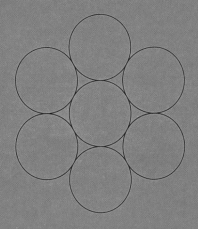

9

SEVEN CHAKRA MANDALA
MY WHEELS OF ENERGY

What is my energy like today?
What do I experience at each chakra?
How can I balance the chakras?

The History of the Seven Chakra Mandala

When a ray of light passes through a prism, the light disperses into a spectrum of seven colours. Similarly, the divine ray of light disperses and is embodied in human beings in the seven chakras. This lesson will serve as an introduction to the seven primary chakras. In this overview we will look at our chakras and try to identify which ones are dominant and which are more passive, which ones are confused and which are well-ordered. Each of the next seven lessons will focus on a different chakra.

I recommend preparing a playlist in advance, with appropriate music for each chakra (as described below), and a variety of art supplies: pencils, felt pens, oil pastels, gouache and watercolour paints. You can write the focus sentences on index cards. Now draw the template for the Seven Chakra Mandala. Read the focus sentences for each chakra. Then read or listen to the guided meditation.

Afterwards put on the playlist and spend ten minutes working on each of the chakras in turn. When the music changes, move on to the next chakra. Let your intuition guide you regarding the colours and techniques to use in each chakra. After you have finished, look at the mandala you have created. The mandala gives us a chance to look at ourselves from a slightly higher perspective. It shows us a picture of our energy centres. It is good to draw this mandala when you are feeling pressured or tense. It balances and calms, gives us a feeling of control, confidence and flow, and helps release blockages.

When you have finished drawing the mandala, step back and take an overall look. Which chakras did you enjoy painting and which ones were more difficult to relate to? Did the painting flow or were you at a loss as to what to draw? Did you go from one chakra to the next easily? Which techniques did you use for each chakra? We can look at each chakra separately, all the chakras together or the chakras in relation to one another. For example, the Third and Fifth Chakras represent the male power within us. Do they appear balanced with the Second, Fourth and Sixth Chakras that represent feminine power? Is the mandala as a whole balanced or do some parts dominate? Does it radiate power and strong energy or is it weak and understated?

Focus Sentences for Each Chakra

First Chakra: Base or Root Chakra

Located at the base of the spine, the Root Chakra is red. This chakra is responsible for the basic life instinct and is associated with words like: rootedness, stability, survival and self-acceptance.

"I am a link in a long chain of parents and children. I grow in a warm home that teaches me to be part of the fabric of humanity. My soul is secure in the body in which it dwells."

Second Chakra: Sacral Chakra

Located under the belly button, the Second Chakra is orange. It is responsible for our sexuality and creativity and is associated with words like: change, sexuality, sensuality, passion and strong emotions.

"In a dualistic world, male and female poles complement and are attracted to each other through sensuality. I discover the creation of life in the movement and flow between my male side and my female side."

Third Chakra: Solar Plexus Chakra

Located above the bellybutton, the Third Chakra is yellow. Words associated with this chakra are: recognition of my self-worth, reason, action, willpower and self-actualization.

"I sit on my golden throne and above me the sun glows, adorning my head like a royal crown."

Fourth Chakra: Heart Chakra

Located in the centre of the chest near the heart, the colour of this chakra is green and pink. Pink represents pure love and green represents giving and receiving. The words associated with this chakra are: emotion, compassion, softness, unconditional love and balance.

"I love myself and honour all men, whatever their path, with compassion. I give to all who need and receive from the world with joy and love."

Fifth Chakra: Throat Chakra

Located in the centre of the throat, the Throat Chakra is blue. Words associated with this chakra are: communication with myself and my surroundings, expression, responsibility, truth, belief, discernment and the ability to judge.

"I am connected to the divine will expressed through me. I am aware of the creative force that brings things from potential to manifestation with love."

Sixth Chakra: Third Eye Chakra

Located between the eyebrows, its colour is violet or indigo. Words associated with this chakra are: imagination, intuition, extrasensory perception, inspiration, spirituality and awareness.

"I close my eyes and create imaginary worlds. I know to read the symbols, colours and shapes that appear in my mind's eye and illuminate my unique path."

Seventh Chakra: Crown Chakra

Located at the crown of the head, its colour is white and gold. The words associated with this chakra are: spirituality, insight, cosmic consciousness, infinite and connection to higher worlds.

"Through the opening in my head, I surrender to the pure divine energy that fills me with infinite love and nourishes me at each and every moment."

Music for the Seven Chakras

The background music for when you are drawing the mandala should be prepared in advance. You can make a playlist of musical tracks, about ten minutes for each chakra. Of course, you can also draw the mandala without listening to special music.

- First Chakra: Aboriginal, drums, and didgeridoo.
- Second Chakra: Belly dancing music or sensual Brazilian music.
- Third Chakra: Rhythmic Indian male singing, expressing power and resolution.
- Fourth Chakra: Quiet and harmonious harp music with background of flowing water.
- Fifth Chakra: Harmonious, soft vocal music.
- Sixth Chakra: New Age music; for example, background music for yoga and reiki treatments.
- Seventh Chakra: Mystical music; for example, the chanting of monks.

Seven Chakra Meditation

Sit in a comfortable position on a chair or pillow; make sure your spine is erect but relaxed. Imagine a ring connected to a taut string at the crown of your head pulling your spine upward, creating space, letting your lungs open wide. Close your eyes and focus on your breathing. Air enters, air exits. With each exhale, release all the tension in your body. Take seven deep breaths. Concentrate on the air that enters and exits your body. Tightly tense the muscles of your eyes, lips, shoulders, arms, hands, buttocks, abdomen, legs and feet. Then relax each body part, one after the other. Repeat this tensing and relaxing.

As you breathe quietly, imagine a thread of light beginning its journey within your body. The thread of light changes its colour depending on which chakra area it is in: red, orange, yellow, green/pink, blue, violet and white.

Look with your mind's eye at the length of coloured thread you have created and try to connect the colours in a harmonious sequence, balanced in one vibrational frequency. If a particular colour is too strong, try to bring it into balance with the other colours. If a colour is too pale, imagine it becoming stronger. Continue until there is harmony.

Slowly return to the feeling of here and now and open your eyes. Move on to the drawing of the mandala.

HOW TO DRAW THE MANDALA

① Open the compass to a radius of 3cm (1½in) and place the compass point on the centre of the page. Draw a circle around this point. Draw a vertical line parallel to the edges of the paper that passes through point 0 and extends beyond the circle's top and bottom perimeters.

② Place the point of the compass at point 1 and mark points 3, to the right, and 4, to the left. Place the point of the compass at point 2 and mark points 5, to the right, and 6, to the left.

③ Draw a long line between points 3 and 6, and between points 4 and 5.

4

With the same radius size, place the compass at point 1 and mark point 7 on the vertical diameter line. Place the compass point at point 4 and mark point 8.

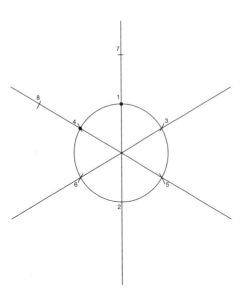

5

Place the compass point at point 6 and mark point 9 on the diagonal line, and place the compass on point 2 and mark point 10 on the vertical diameter line.

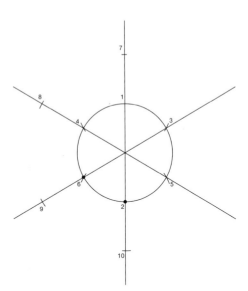

6

Place the compass point at point 5 and mark point 11. Place the compass point at point 3 and mark point 12.

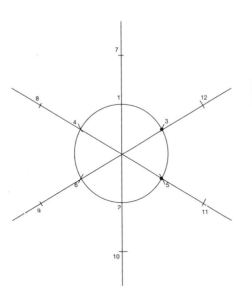

7

Place the compass point at each point from 7 to 12, and at each point draw a circle with a radius of 3cm (1½in).

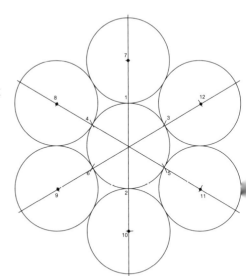

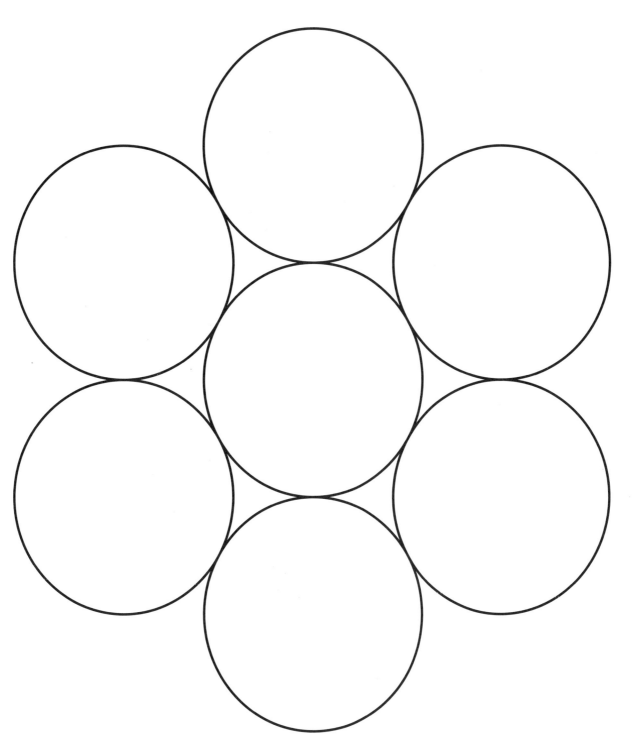

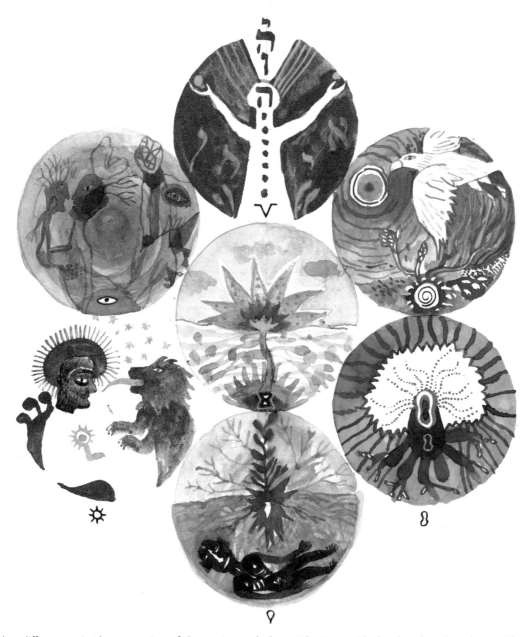

Notice the difference in the energies of the various chakras. The Base Chakra has harsh colours. The person is lying limply, powerlessly, pointing to a block in the life force. However, the Heart Chakra is blossoming with a lotus flower in the middle of a lake. In the centre there is love and tranquility ... for the time being.

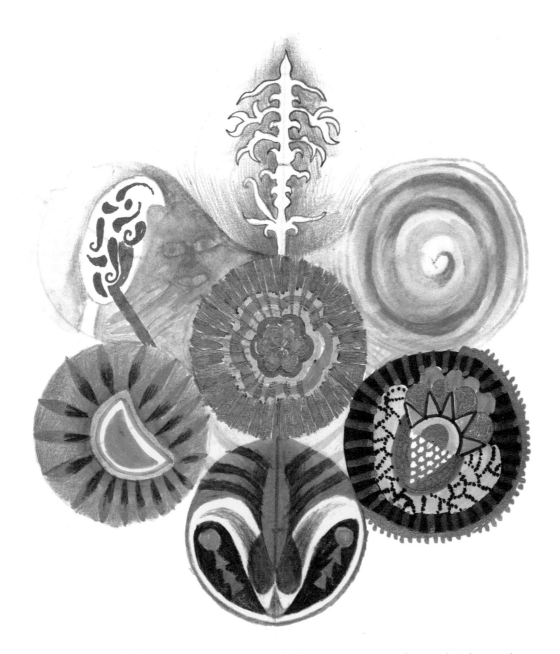

The circles of these chakras seem more balanced. They are connected to each other and create a continuity that radiates calm, strength and power. When we draw the Seven Chakra Mandala, additional layers of the soul are revealed.

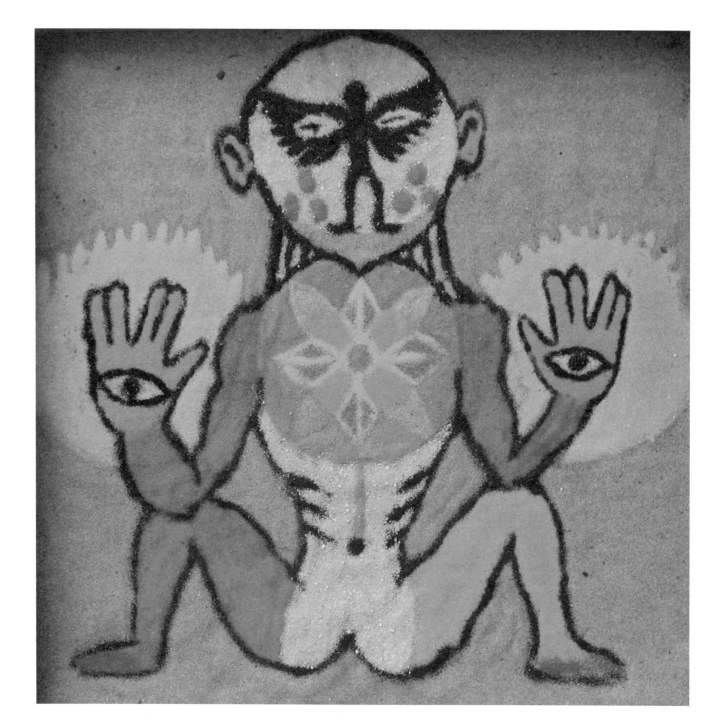

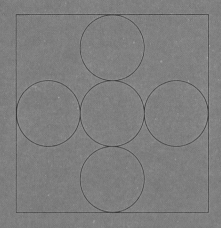

10

ROOT CHAKRA MANDALA
THE GATEWAY TO THIS WORLD

Do I accept my body's limitations?
From what base did I begin my life?
What tribal identity and family heritage was I born into?

The History of the Root Chakra Mandala

The First Chakra, the Root Chakra, is related in Hebrew to the words for red, earth, blood and man. This chakra focuses on the moment of the soul's union with matter – the beginning of life, the moment of conception from which we continue to grow and develop. This chakra expresses the experience of *tzimtzum* (contraction) and choice. We can compare the process of *tzimtzum* to the building of a character in a play who is given a personality, physical characteristics, special qualities, a place and a time. The soul enters a particular role in this world in a body that is created from the birth family's unique gene pool. This gene pool determines the person's health, basic personality traits and intelligence level. In addition, this person is born into a historical period, location and culture, with its own particular customs, art and language. They first experience a passage through the gate of birth into a body that exists in the physical dimension. The infant stage is characterized by helplessness and complete dependence on parents. This is a significant period for building a sense of trust, confidence and groundedness. The Root Chakra is associated with childhood and the provision of a stable foundation for future growth.

The best way to connect to the Root Chakra is by working in sand. The touch of the sand connects us to the biblical quote, "... for dust thou art, and unto dust shalt thou return" (Genesis 3:20). The mandala draws us closer to the understanding that we are like structures made of sand – temporary and unique. There will never be someone exactly like us in the world.

Creating a sand mandala gives the feeling of a slow but constant flow that cannot be stopped. We allow the creation to be built, to be, to change and to disappear. Like the non-permanent nature of sand, the mandala also comes into being and then disappears. So we, too, are temporarily present in the material world, undergoing continuous change. Creating a sand mandala allows us to be here and now, observing change and accepting it with love. The feel of the sand in our hands returns us to our childhood, to being directly in touch with the earth, nature and the joy of playing. We connect to memories of infancy and childhood, to a lack of control. You cannot control sand because it has its own inner movement. You can only join in the movement.

The process of creating a sand mandala allows us to be more authentic. A creation in sand is ephemeral. It cannot be preserved and so we will not be admired for it. This is a process that takes place in the here and now. While we work, we gather and impart our energy and when we dismantle the mandala we release this energy with all the blessings that were generated into the world. This energy will be recycled and will return to us renewed. We can create the Root Chakra mandala from coloured sand on top of soft beach sand, on a mound of earth in the garden, in a forest clearing or at home in a sandbox.

The sand mandala connects to robustness, health and physical sensations. It bestows a feeling of self-confidence, grounding and abundance. When we finish the mandala we can look at it and ask ourselves questions. From what base did I begin my life? What kind of family and circumstances was I born into? What culture and customs did I grow up with? What colours, sounds and smells accompanied me at the beginning of my journey? This is the time to recall our earliest memories and to send healing to places that have yet to be healed.

Dismantling the Mandala

After contemplating our mandala and receiving its messages, it is important to experience the stage of dismantling with a feeling of release. The process of dismantling will help us to accept the fact of our own temporal existence in the world. We can look again at the mandala that we have created in the sand and send ourselves blessings of healing, love and abundance. We can send a blessing to someone else as well. We push the sand carefully from the edges toward the centre, letting the colours blend together. We then gather it in a bag and scatter it into the sea. If we create our mandala far from a body of water, we can bury the sand in a hole we dig in the earth. This way, our blessings for ourselves and others will spread throughout the world.

Preparing a Sand Box

Either build or order a square wooden box 40 × 40 x 5cm (15½ x 15½ x 2in). This size is suited to working at home on a table. If you have an outside patio or yard, you can build a larger sandbox. I recommend getting a Perspex cover that can protect the sand and let you work on the mandala over time until you reach the dismantling stage.

Collect earth and sand of various colours from different areas in plastic bottles. If it is not available locally, sand can be purchased and mixed with coloured pigments. Fill a 1.5L (3 pint) plastic soft drink or water bottle with sand and pour it into a large bowl. Add a tablespoon of coloured pigment. Mix the ingredients with a large spoon, using a funnel to return the coloured sand to the plastic bottle. When working with children, make sure that you use non-toxic pigments. For instance, blend the sand with non-toxic gouache paint, let it dry and crush it into powder. When you sit down to work, pour the coloured sand into small bowls.

To make the mandala in the sandbox, first cut out a circle with a 12cm (4½in) diameter from cardboard. Pour two cups of natural sand over the bottom of the tray. Start to play with the sand, like a child: feel the sand in your hands, pour it between your fingers, gather it together and scatter it again. Then spread the sand uniformly all over the sand tray and pack it down. Place the cardboard circle down and trace around it, thus marking the template in the sand. Now intuitively choose one of the bowls of coloured sand. Take a pinch of the sand between your thumb, index and middle fingers and let it trickle through your fingers in the centre of the mandala, marking the bindu. Continue to use this technique to create the mandala, working from the centre outwards toward the periphery of the circle.

Working in sand allows us to create freely, without worrying about being precise. You can also work in three dimensions by making depressions in the sand or piling it up. To create stronger colours, hold your hand as close as possible to the sandbox. To create lighter colours, release the sand from further away. Experiment with the movement of your hands as you release the sand to create different effects.

Root Chakra Meditation

Sit in a comfortable position on a chair or pillow; make sure your spine is erect but relaxed. Imagine a ring connected to a taut string at the crown of your head pulling your spine upward, creating space, letting your lungs open wide. Close your eyes and focus on your breathing. Air enters, air exits. With each exhale, release all the tension in your body. Take seven deep breaths. Concentrate on the air that enters and exits your body. Tightly tense the muscles of your eyes, lips, shoulders, arms, hands, buttocks, abdomen, legs and feet. Then relax each body part, one after the other. Repeat this tensing and relaxing.

Breathe softly and regularly. Return to the time before you were born. Imagine yourself as a soul that has chosen to reincarnate into the material world in your body. According to Jewish belief, the foetus knows everything while in the mother's womb, but a short time before birth an angel comes and taps it gently above the upper lip, causing total forgetfulness of all that was known. We are supposed to rediscover this knowledge during our lifetime. Thus the soul knows and chooses the family, the ethnic group and the country into which they will be born. We come into the material world to undergo healing and redemption, and all that we experience in our lifetime has meaning. We ask ourselves: what is our tikkun – what do we need to change or heal – in this lifetime? It is not easy to get clear, precise answers, but we can allow ourselves to ponder the question and see what arises.

Slowly and gently open your eyes and move on to creating the Root Chakra Mandala with coloured sand or on paper.

HOW TO DRAW THE MANDALA

1

Open the compass to a radius of 3cm (1½in) and place the compass point on the centre of the page. Draw a circle around this point and mark a vertical line parallel to the edges of the paper that passes through point 0 and extends beyond the circle's top and bottom perimeter. Mark points 1 and 2 where the line crosses the circle.

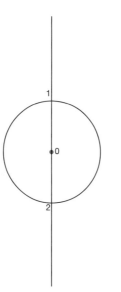

2

Place the compass point at point 1 and mark points 3, to the right, and 4, to the left. Place the compass point at point 2 and mark points 5, to the right, and 6, to the left.

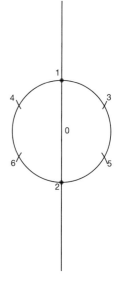

3

Place the compass point at point 3 and draw a small arc opposite point 0. Place the compass point at point 5 and draw a small arc that intersects the previous arc at point 7. Connect points 0 and 7 by drawing a long line that extends beyond the circle to the right and left, and mark points 8 and 9.

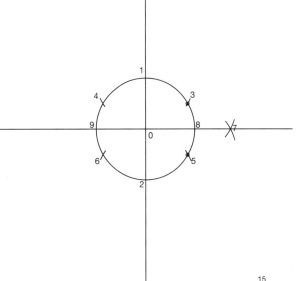

4

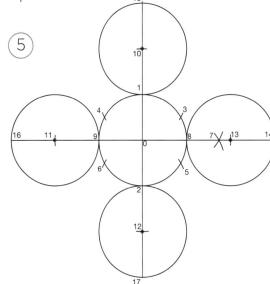

Place the compass point at point 1 and mark where the 3cm (1½in) radius intersects the vertical line – point 10. Repeat this, placing the compass point at points 8, 2 and 9 and marking points 11, 12 and 13.

5

Draw a circle with a 3cm (1½in) radius at points 10, 11, 12 and 13 and mark points 14, 15, 16 and 17 on the drawing.

(6)

Place the compass point at 14 and open the compass radius to point 0. Draw a small arc above and below from points 14 and 16. Placing the compass point at 15 and 17, draw an arc to the right and left. Mark the intersections A, B, C and D.

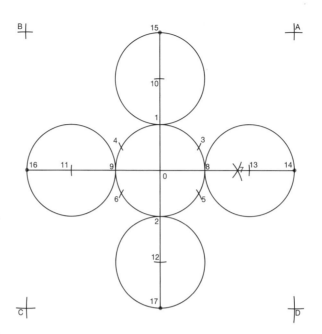

(7)

Connect the points A, B, C and D, forming a square.

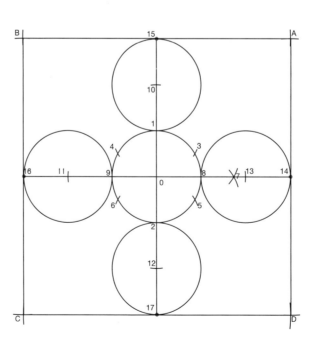

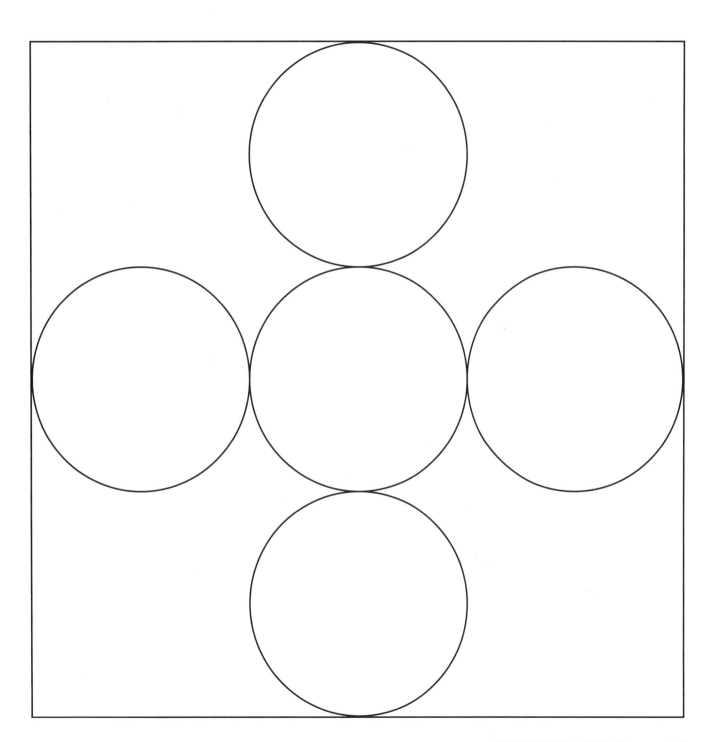

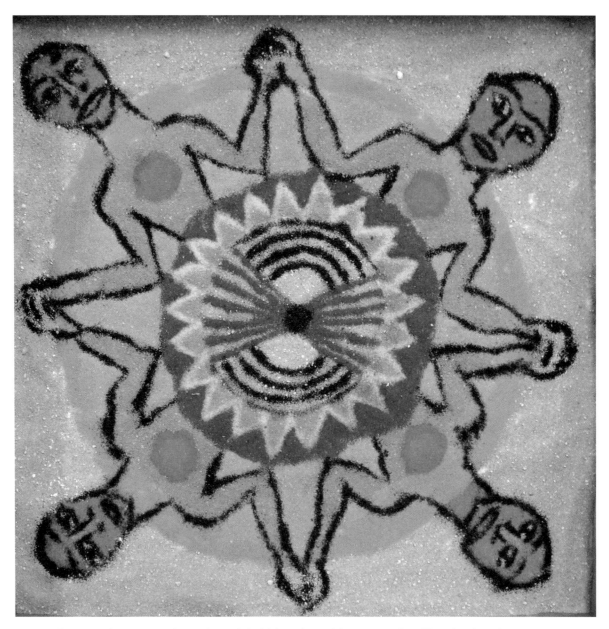

Four figures, drawn in coloured sand, hold hands and form a circle of brotherhood, support and respect for one another. Their message is that we must be humble since we come from dust and return to dust. This circle of people connects me to my need to belong.

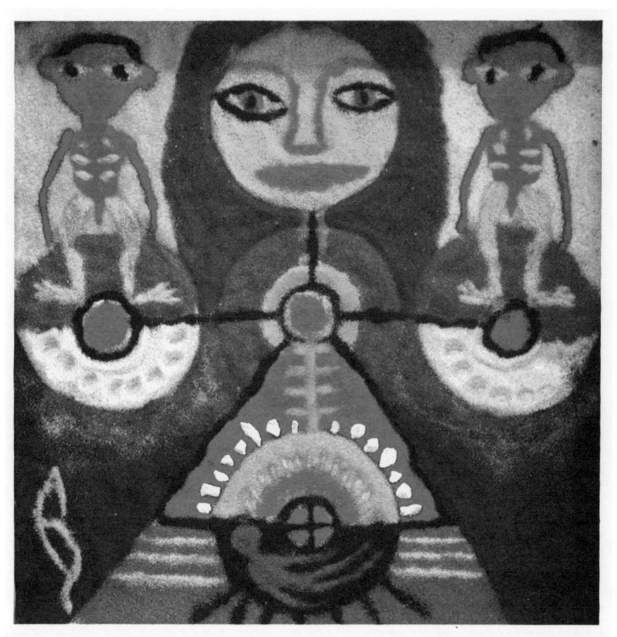

Working in sand returns me to primary connections from the past. This mandala describes my connection to my mother. A large woman with big breasts and a womb is reminiscent of an earth goddess. The triangular body radiates stability and groundedness. The figure is containing and loving, her face is full of light and her heart is wide. Her hands are outstretched, holding me and my brother.

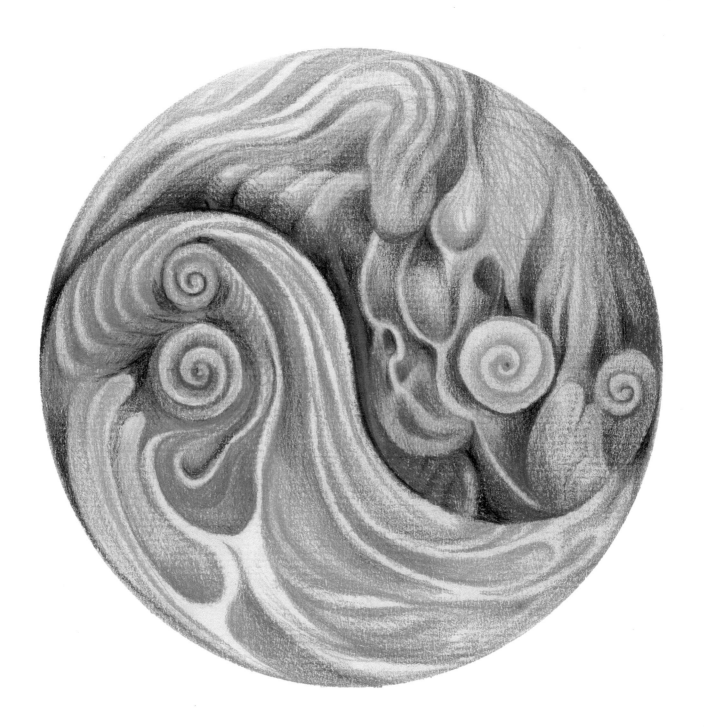

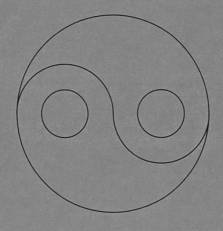

11

SACRAL CHAKRA MANDALA

DESIRE AND CREATION

What is life?
How do I connect to the power of creation?
What is masculine and what is feminine within me?

The History of the Sacral Chakra Mandala

The colour of the Second Chakra – the chakra of desire and creation – is orange. It is connected to the element of water and located below the bellybutton. This chakra focuses on our feeling of being present in the world. The baby looks around, asks himself what kind of world he has come to, and discovers that it is a dualistic world. We take form in a masculine or feminine body, but both polarities exist within us and are always trying to connect. The attraction of these poles and the constant movement between them is the force that fuels creation in all areas and keeps us open to new ideas.

Creation is the essence of life. Life continually moves between two polarities. For example, the yin yang symbol comprises two waves of opposite colours, black yin and white yang within a circle, with each side containing a small circle of the opposite colour. The concept of yin and yang comes from ancient Chinese philosophy and describes two primal, opposing, yet perfect forces that are found in constant motion in all things in the universe.

Yin is described as the cold, short, dark part of the process; it is associated with earth and winter. The moon sailing in the dark night heavens symbolizes feminine nature, related to dreams and intuition. Yang is the hot, tall, fast, active and illuminated part. Yang is related to the light of day and the glow of the sun, symbolizing masculine nature, the heavens and summer.

The simple meaning of yang in Chinese is "the light side of the mountain", thus connected to daytime activity. Yin means "the dark side of the mountain" and relates to night and cold. Yin and yang can also be used to describe processes at different stages of transformation. For example, cold water is yin; when we boil it we change it to steam and yang.

The encounter between masculine and feminine in the world is not only expressed in the encounter between men and women. In a much wider sense, it is the meeting of opposites – between daylight and night, for instance. Sunrise and sunset are moments when two forces meet, and this merging creates a sense of connection. The biblical Song of Songs describes the love of men and women, and has been interpreted as meaning the love of God for his creations.

Desire is the force that connects a man and a woman and the connection between them is the act of creation. The encounter between opposites is similar to the act of breathing – to inhaling and exhaling – or to the flow of waves alternately approaching and falling back from the shore.

The Sacral Chakra mandala develops creativity. It balances and quiets the soul and renews movement and flow into blocked areas. It elicits enthusiasm, health, harmony and creative joy.

After drawing the Sacral Chakra mandala, we can look at it and notice how we related to the two polarities. Did we spend more time on one side or the other? How did we draw the masculine side? The feminine side? This is an opportunity to look at the balance between the two poles and their interrelationship.

Sacral Chakra Meditation

Sit in a comfortable position on a chair or pillow; make sure your spine is erect but relaxed. Imagine a ring connected to a taut string at the crown of your head pulling your spine upward, creating space, letting your lungs open wide. Close your eyes and focus on your breathing. Air enters, air exits. With each exhale, release all the tension in your body. Take seven deep breaths. Concentrate on the air that enters and exits your body. Tightly tense the muscles of your eyes, lips, shoulders, arms, hands, buttocks, abdomen, legs and feet. Then relax each body part, one after the other. Repeat this tensing and relaxing.

As you breathe quietly and regularly, imagine a line of white light that starts at the crown of your head and continues downwards, dividing your body into the right side and the left side. The right side symbolizes the masculine, and the left side the feminine. Observe what arises from each side – sounds, voices, sights, feelings, images – as you place your attention first on one side of your body and then on the other. Open your hands. Imagine that an image, representing your masculine side, rests on your right hand, and that on your left hand sits an image of your feminine side. What does each hand hold: an animal, an object, a figure, a characteristic, a landscape, a feeling? Finally place your hands together over your heart and let the images meet. Imagine the encounter and the conversation between them.

Gently, return to the feeling of here and now. Open your eyes and begin to draw the mandala.

HOW TO DRAW THE MANDALA

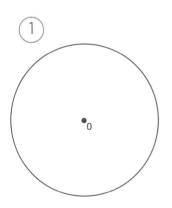

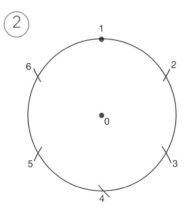

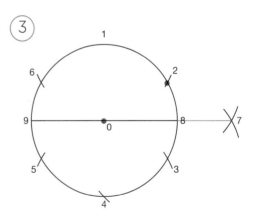

Open the compass to a radius of 9cm (3½in) and place the compass point on the centre of the page. Draw a circle around this point.

Place the compass point on the top of the circle, at point 1. Divide the circle into six equal parts using the compass radius and mark points 2–6.

Place the compass point at point 2 and mark a small arc opposite 0. Place the compass point at point 3 and draw a small arc that intersects the previous arc at point 7. Using a ruler, connect point 7 to point 0, and mark line 8–9.

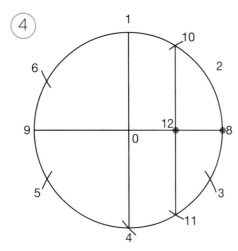

(4)

Place the point of the compass (with the same radius opening) at point 8 and mark above and below on the circle, points 10 and 11. Using a ruler, connect points 10 and 11 and mark point 12 on line 8–9. (Point 12 marks the half-radius point.)

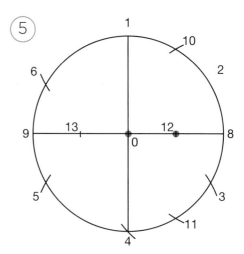

(5)

Decrease the size of the radius to the distance between point 0 and point 12. Place the compass point at point 0, and mark point 13.

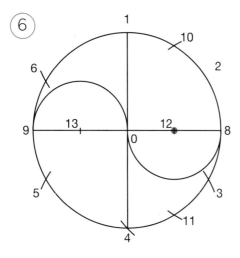

(6)

Place the compass point at point 12 and draw a half circle from points 0–8. Place the compass at point 13 and draw a half circle from points 0–9.

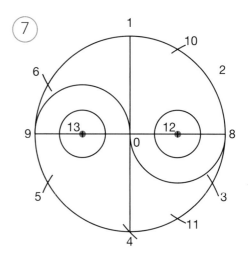

(7)

Fix the compass radius at 1.5cm (½in). Place the compass point at point 12 and draw a circle. Place the compass point at point 13 and draw a circle.

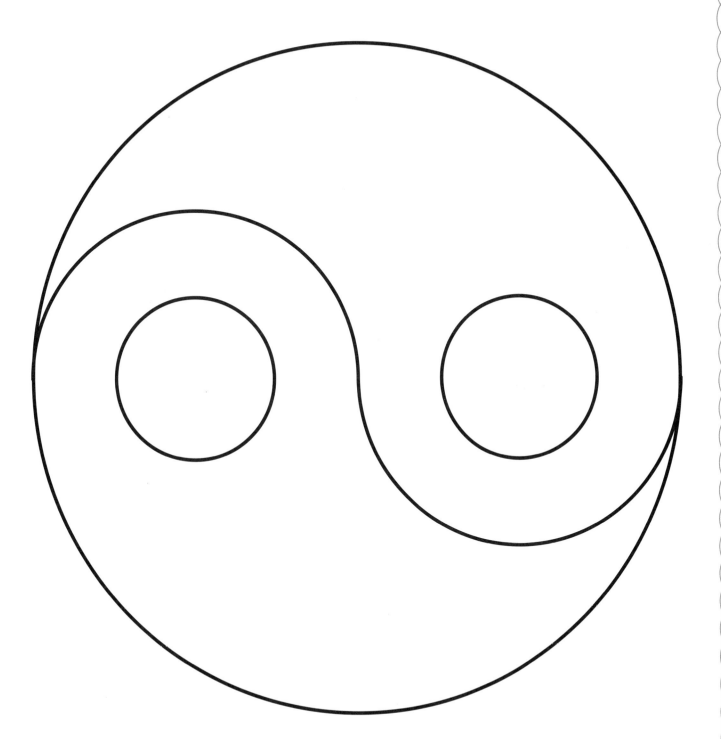

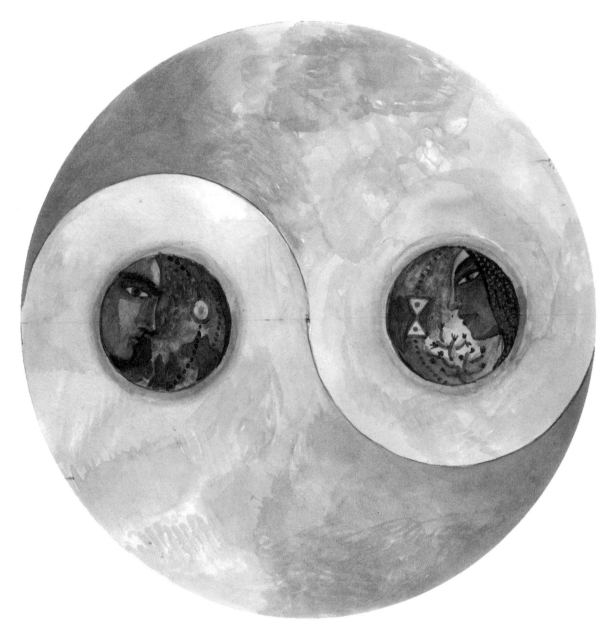

Two figures, a man and a woman, live in existential loneliness. They do not make contact with one another; each one lives in their own private world. We peek at them through a small, round window that looks like an opening in a submarine, protected by thick, impenetrable glass.

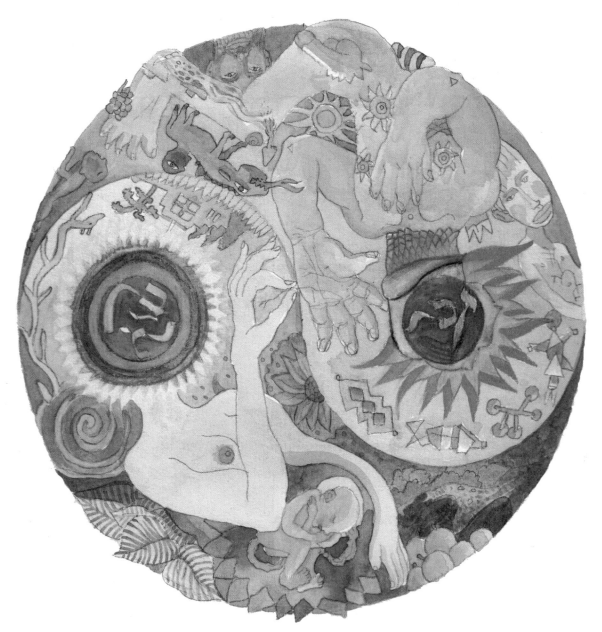

The male and the female live in cooperation. There is an intimate connection all along the clear border between them, and the two parts of the mandala warmly embrace each other. Each side is complete by itself but empowered by the connection between them. In the centre of the mandala, at the connecting point, the woman touches the lifeline on the man's hand.

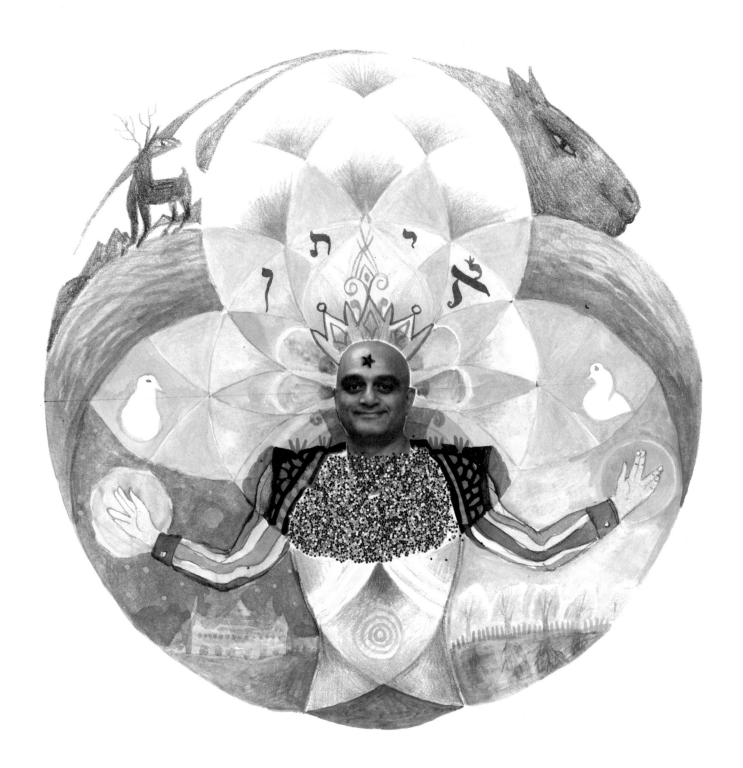

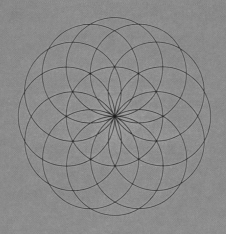

12

SOLAR PLEXUS CHAKRA MANDALA
THE INNER KINGDOM

Do I honour my presence in the world?
What does my royal throne look like?
Who am I and what is my purpose?

The History of the Solar Plexus Chakra Mandala

The colour of the Third Chakra, located between the bellybutton and the diaphragm, is yellow. It is associated with the element of fire and masculine energy. In the Second Chakra we focused on the meaning of life's essence by looking at life and its cyclical movement between polarities. In the Third Chakra, we examine who we are: what is the purpose and meaning of my life? What qualities do I possess that shine like the sun, and which should I use as I play my part in the human mandala? Each one of us was born with a role and an inner kingdom which we are meant to realize in this life. Only when we recognize and connect to this kingdom can we fully experience and be satisfied with our inner and outer worlds.

The Third Chakra is the helm and the royal rod which represents our powers of leadership in directing our abilities and in recognizing our self-worth. This is the tool that allows us to be aware of the role we are supposed to play in this incarnation. Yellow is the colour associated with consciousness and thought, the colour that enables people to see, act and express their capabilities in the world. Thus it is necessary to first take care of ourselves before we can be an enlightened ruler. In the biblical story about the relationship between David, son of Jesse, and King Saul, it describes Saul as being gripped by terrible jealousy, bitterness and depression when the youthful David wins great success and love. As long as we are not full within ourselves, we will look at the world outside with jealousy like Saul. This is a source of anger. Only when we know that the world is an infinite source of appreciation and acceptance can we feel tranquil on our own throne.

The Third Chakra is located in the abdomen, just under the ribs, at a place named the solar plexus. According to Chinese medicine, this is the source of life energy, or Chi – the energy of power, initiative, movement and action. When drawing the mandala associated with the solar plexus, we focus on our sense of self-worth. We concentrate on questions of motivation, significance and understanding. What motivates us to act? What meaning does our presence have in the world? Our sense of self-worth is related to the trust we have for the power existing within us.

The words associated with this chakra are fire, sun, gold and royalty. Fire is the source of energy; it is constantly in motion. The inner fire is what lights our way in the world. The sun, the star of fire, represents the power that moves and activates life. The sun rules the kingdom of day, the visible and the external. Gold is considered the most expensive and precious of metals. Chemically resistant to outside elements, it is renowned for its stable and eternal quality. Every person is the ruler of their life and of the course of their inner realm.

Modern life has distanced us from the element of fire. The fear of fire and the threat it poses have caused us to keep away from it. Before drawing the mandala, I recommend returning to the ancient closeness with the fire element by looking into a flame. You can light a campfire in a field or a fire in a fireproof container in the yard. During the drawing it is good to light a candle and place it in the centre of the table. The template I chose to represent the Third Chakra is inspired by the golden emblem of King Louis XIV of France, who called himself the Sun King. His face is in the centre of the emblem, surrounded by the sun's rays. Similar to King Louis, we shall honour ourselves in a royal mandala, fit for our inner king or queen. I suggest you have your picture taken for this mandala. Then cut out the photo in a circle and place it in the centre of the mandala. Use shiny, gold-coloured materials, such as gold dust, gold paper, markers and acrylic colours that glow and shine.

After drawing the mandala in honour of our inner kingdom, contemplate it and see what king or queen you have chosen to draw and what kingdom they rule. Take note of any feelings that arise and how you relate to the image of yourself that you have placed in the centre of the mandala.

Solar Plexus Meditation

Find a quiet, ventilated space where you feel comfortable; you may want to light a candle or incense and/or turn on soft music in the background.

Sit in a comfortable position on a chair or pillow; make sure your spine is erect but relaxed. Imagine a ring connected to a taut string at the crown of your head pulling your spine upward, creating space, letting your lungs open wide. Close your eyes and focus on your breathing. Air enters, air exits. With each exhale, release all the tension in your body. Take seven deep breaths. Concentrate on the air that enters and exits your body. Tightly tense the muscles of your eyes, lips, shoulders, arms, hands, buttocks, abdomen, legs and feet. Then relax each body part, one after the other. Repeat this tensing and relaxing.

Place your hands one on the other in the centre of your abdomen above your bellybutton. Look at the candle's flame. Feel the energy of the fire. Close your eyes and imagine yourself in a spacious, well-lit room with an elaborately adorned throne just for you in the centre. Concentrate on the details of the throne and then sit down on it. Feel the power, self-respect, honour and presence that ensue. Observe the world from a quiet, safe and secure place.

Slowly return to the feeling of being present, here and now. Open your eyes. Look again at the candle's flame and keep the feeling of being royalty.

HOW TO DRAW THE MANDALA

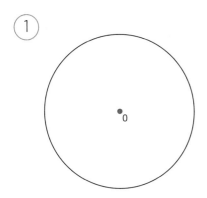

① Open the compass to a radius of 3.5cm (1½in) and place the compass point on the centre of the page. Draw a circle around this point.

② Place the compass point on the top of the circle, at point 1. Using the same radius, divide the circle into six equal parts and mark points 2–6.

③ Place the compass point at point 2 and mark a small arc opposite 0. Place the compass point at point 3, intersect the arc with another arc and mark it point 7. Using a ruler, connect point 7 to point 0 and mark points 8–9.

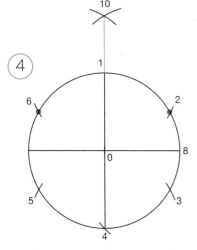

④ Repeat step 3 to create a line between points 1 and 4. Place the compass point at points 2 and 6 to create the intersecting point 10.

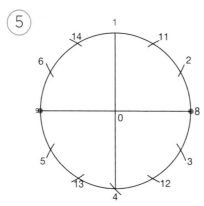

⑤ Place the point of the compass (with the same radius opening) on point 8 and mark points 10 and 11 on the circle. Place the compass on point 9 and mark points 12 and 13.

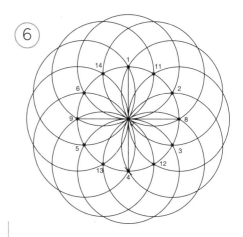

⑥ From each point on the circle, draw a new circle with the same radius.

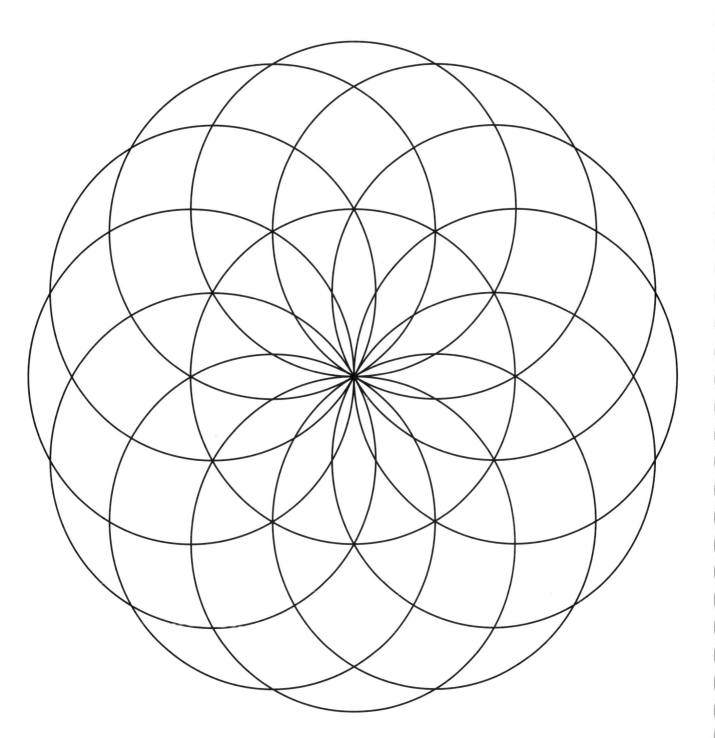

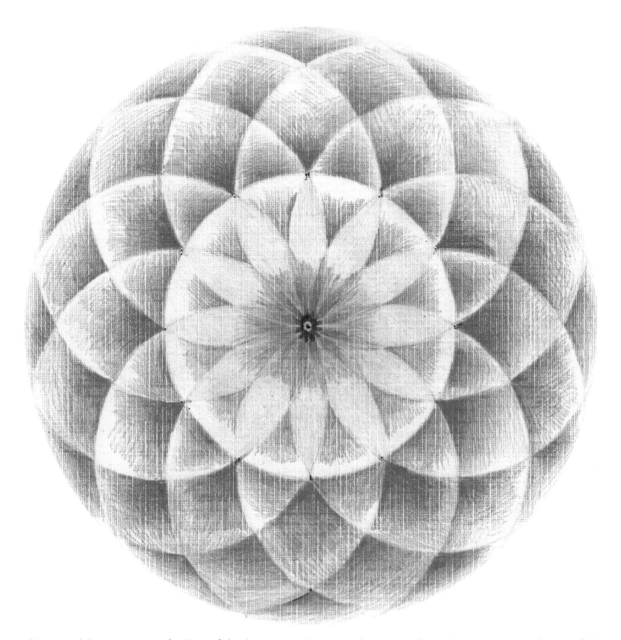

This mandala gives me a feeling of the heart opening, gentleness and sensitivity. It reminds me of the lotus flower that blooms in water. When I draw the element of water in the mandala template that represents fire, I balance and calm my dramas and strong passions. This enables me to relax from the struggles in my everyday life and give myself a hug.

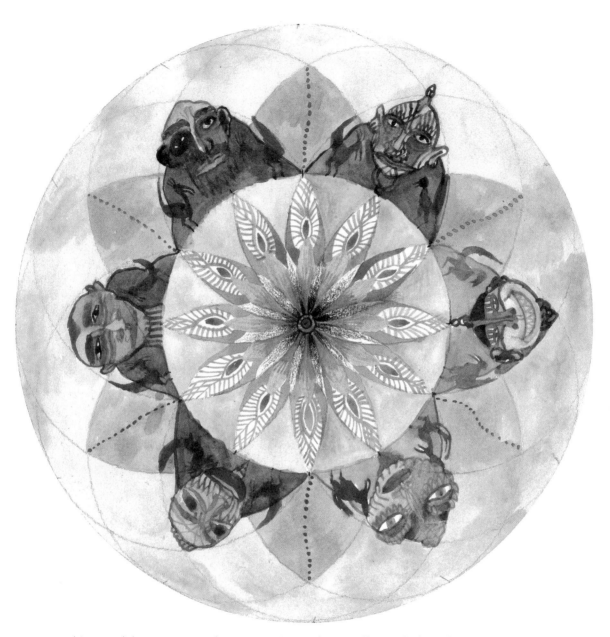

For me, this mandala represents the aggressive and controlling side found in the masculine within me. The burning yellow colour in the background represents looking outwardly, and the need to receive validation from external sources. The figures sitting in the circle look like a forum of policymakers who are planning to join forces to control and rule.

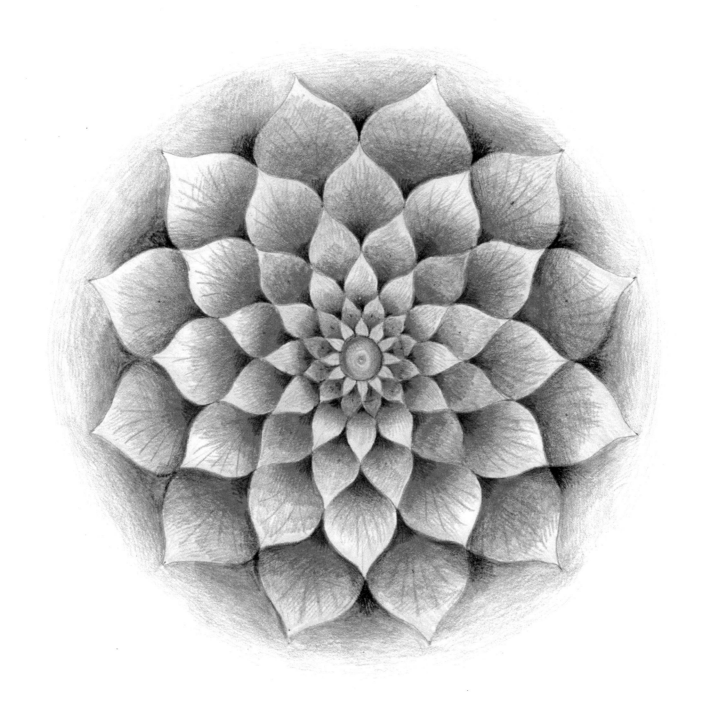

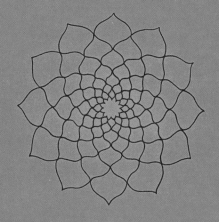

13

HEART CHAKRA MANDALA
UNCONDITIONAL LOVE

Do we have the ability to really listen to one another?
How much compassion do we have for the suffering of others?
Do we feel the joy of giving?

The History of the Heart Chakra Mandala

The primary colour of the Heart Chakra is green, and its secondary colour is pink. The Sanskrit name is Anahata, the eternally beating drum. At this centre the heavenly white energy meets earthly red energy. Their encounter in the heart creates the colour pink, the colour of love. Green symbolizes the balance between the three lower chakras and the three higher chakras, as the heart is in the middle of the seven chakras. The Heart Chakra is located in the middle of the chest and is associated with the element of air. The heart centre is responsible for our relationships. When the heart is open, we find unconditional love within ourselves, with no expectation for recompense. The three lower chakras express humanity's basic needs and strongly influence our behaviour. When these needs are satisfied, we are open to see others as they are.

More than any other world leader, the Dalai Lama, whose name means "ocean of wisdom", talks of the need for compassion concealed in the Heart Chakra: "As men we are social creatures. We come into the world as a result of other people's actions. We survive through dependence upon others. Whether we like it or not, there are almost no moments in our lives when we are not gaining some benefit from the actions of others. Yet there is nothing extraordinary about the fact that our greatest joy comes when we are motivated by our concern for the well-being of others. However, that's not the whole story. Apparently deeds done to benefit others do not just give us joy; they reduce our experience of suffering. To some degree the compassionate, loving, patient, tolerant and forgiving person recognizes the possible influence of his actions on others and plans his actions accordingly. Thus spiritual work includes action based on concern for the well-being of others. In addition it demands that we transform ourselves to be more willing to act in such a way. Any discussion of spiritual work in terms other than these is meaningless."

The Heart Chakra represents a spiritual step up. It expresses our ability to be aware of ourselves and of others, which requires us to develop our powers of observation and contemplation. Words related to this chakra's qualities are: love, compassion, understanding, listening, giving and receiving. This chakra focuses on our relationship to the world. Its location in the middle of the chest between our two arms expresses our connection to the world through giving and receiving. These are two energies that flow inwards and outwards: the ability to put others in the centre, to listen to their heart's longings and give the love needed on the one hand and, on the other, the ability to open and receive love from another.

Compassion is the way to be attentive to the suffering of another. There is a difference between compassion and pity. When we live in a world of separation, we feel pity for the other person, since we separate ourselves from them and look at them from above. However, if we understand that life is a wheel, we relate to the suffering person with the understanding that, with a wheel's turn, we could be in their situation. Thus we can identify with their suffering, feel compassion and be completely present. Our presence and dedication to the other creates healing possibilities for them.

An open Heart Chakra engenders gratitude for the infinite abundance that flows to us. To increase our sense of freedom, we must recognize the changing, temporal nature of the material world. The more we decrease our attachment to it, the more we can feel our presence in the here and now, compassionately care for ourselves and others, and protect our environment.

When we finish the mandala, we will give it to someone we love. We will ask that person what they see in the mandala and why they think we wanted to give it to them. We will examine our ability to give and our ability to listen deeply. To be completely present and contain another we need to quiet our personal noise, which is an obstacle to really listening to and focusing on the needs of another.

The template for the Heart Mandala is based on the structure of the lotus flower that opens its petals to heavenly light, just as we open to the world to give and receive. Eastern cultures use the lotus flower as a symbol of spiritual development. The roots of the flower are concealed in the muddy earth, symbolizing the material world. From there it grows in the water, symbolizing emotions, and finally it rises up toward the air and light, where the wondrous flower peeks out from within its leaves.

Drawing the Heart Chakra mandala expands the heart's ability to give and receive, to love unconditionally and to open to the needs of others. The mandala fosters love, good partnerships and couplehood, and improves close relationships.

Heart Chakra Meditation

Choose a person to make a mandala for and give as a gift. In order to create a mandala suited to the person you have chosen, you should meet with them prior to doing the mandala. Choose a setting in which they will feel comfortable and be able to express themselves freely. Listen with complete, open attentiveness and non-judgement for at least half an hour. Don't ask leading questions or speak about yourself. Imagine yourself as a container of love that accepts the other person as they are, unconditionally. Internalize what you hear, observe the energy radiating from them. Use this energy to inspire you as you create the mandala for them.

After listening, turn to drawing the lotus flower template for the Heart Chakra mandala.

HOW TO DRAW THE MANDALA

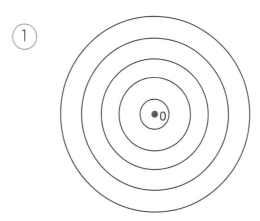

Open the compass to a radius of 1cm (½in) and place the compass point on the centre of the page. draw a circle around this point. Return to point 0 and draw four concentric circles with radiuses of 2cm (⁸/₁₀in), 3.5cm (1½in), 5.5cm (2in) and 8cm (3in).

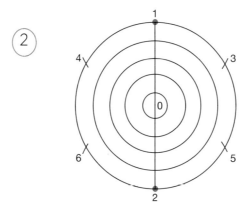

Draw a vertical diameter dividing the circle in half, line 1–2. (Make sure that line 1–2 goes through point 0 and is parallel to the sides of the page.) With the compass open to the last radius of 8cm (3in), place the compass point at 1 and mark the intersecting points on the circle: 3 to the right and 4 to the left. Place the compass point at 2 and mark the intersecting points on the circle: 5 to the right and 6 to the left.

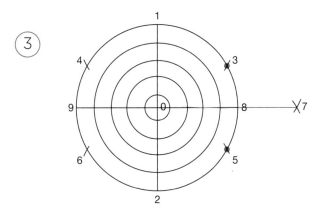

(3)

With the same radius, place the compass point at point 3 and mark a small arc opposite the 0. Place the compass point at point 5 and intersect the arc with another arc and mark it as point 7. Using a ruler, connect point 7 to point 0 and mark line 8–9.

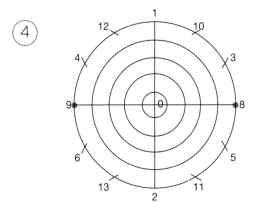

(4)

Place the point of the compass on point 8 and mark points 10 and 11 on the circle. Place the compass on point 9 and mark points 12 and 13.

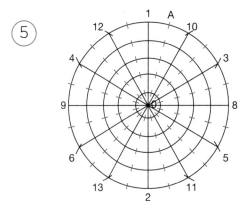

(5)

Using a ruler, draw a line connecting points 11–12, 4–5, 3–6 and 10–13. Each circle is now divided into 12 parts; mark a dotted red line down the middle (judging by eye) of each of the 12 parts, as illustrated.

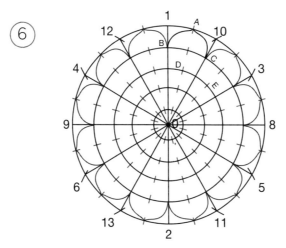

To draw the petal, draw a curved line between point A–B and point A–C as shown in the diagram. Repeat drawing the petals in all the parts of the outer circle.

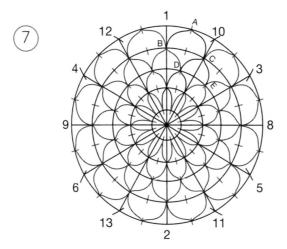

Draw a curved line from point C–D and from point C–E as shown in the diagram. Repeat drawing the petals in all the parts of the second circle. Repeat drawing the petals in the other circles using the same basic instructions.

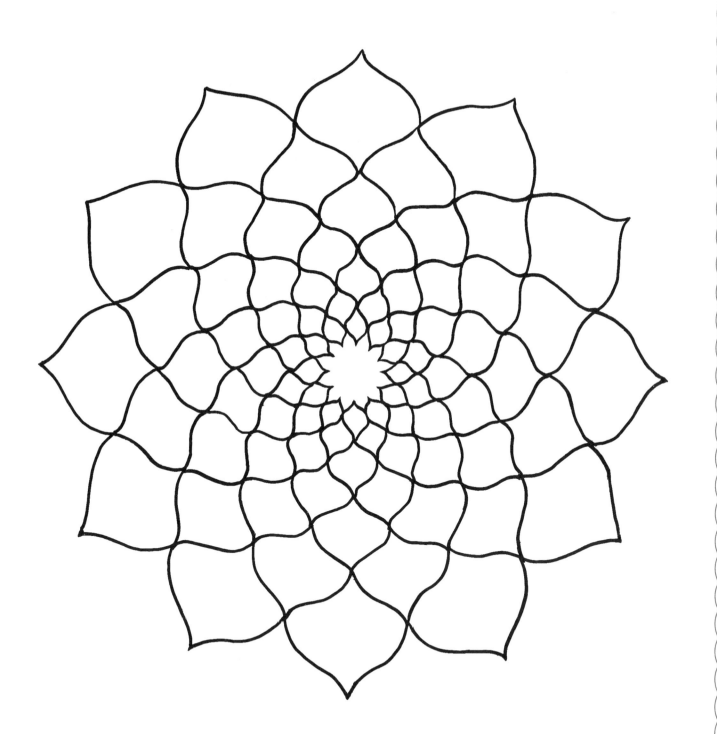

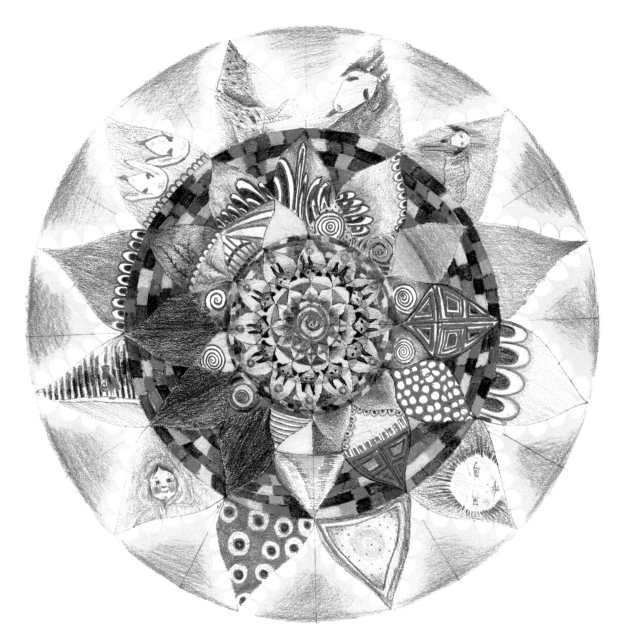

I received this mandala from my friend Anat Rotem. Anat invested time and infinite patience in drawing the tiny details. If we look closely we can discern that each figure tells its personal story. Rich colouring, joy and a world of imagination are joined in harmony. I felt that this was a gift that came from the heart.

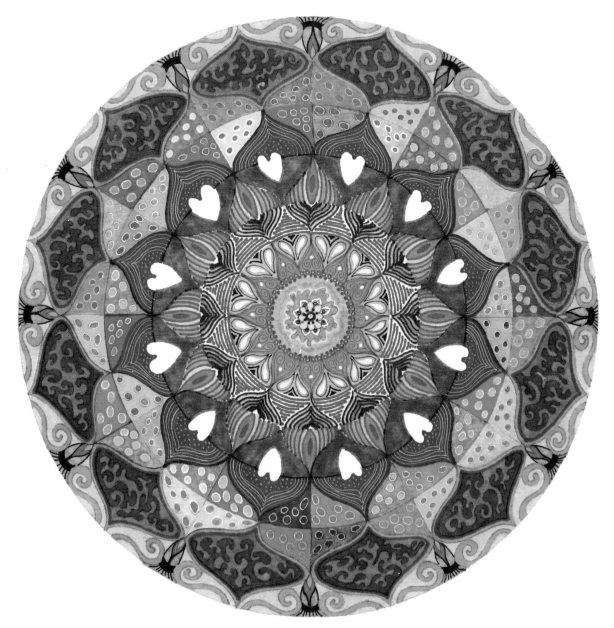

I received this mandala from my friend Ofra Danon. The symmetry, precision and rich colouring give a sense of stability, security and calm. The hearts arranged in a circle look as if they are dancing or sharing in some kind of harmonious group activity. I felt that Ofra was blessing me with acceptance, containment, warmth and hugs.

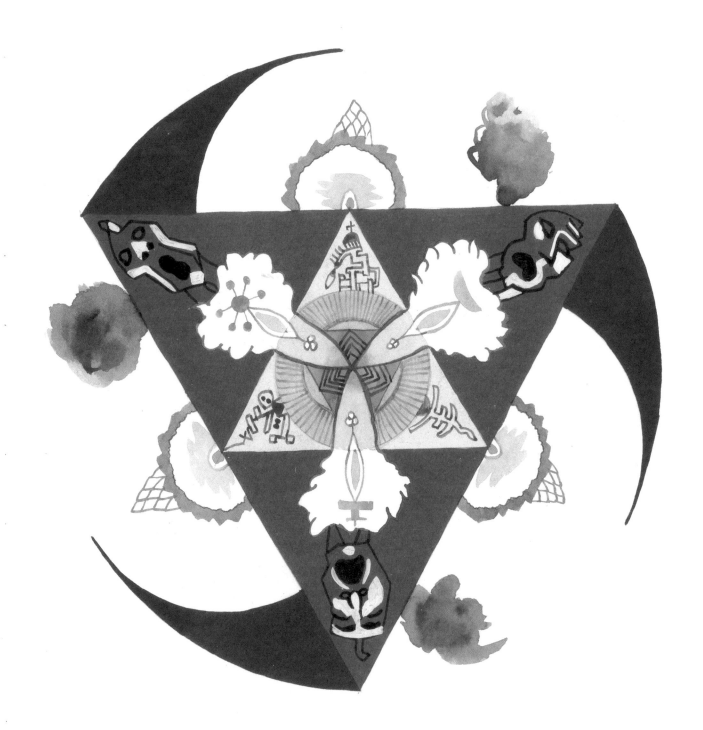

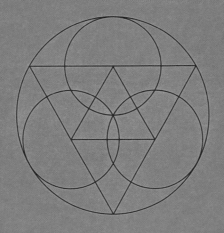

14

THROAT CHAKRA MANDALA
THE POWER OF WORDS

Do I speak the truth?
Do I have the courage to express my truth?
How can I connect my inner world to the world outside?

The History of the Throat Chakra Mandala

Blue is the colour of the Throat Chakra. It lies parallel to the vocal cords in the centre of the throat, allowing it to sharpen our self-expression. The Throat Chakra is primarily related to the conscious use of our mind to communicate with our surroundings. In order to express ourselves clearly and precisely so that others will understand us, we must develop the ability of conscious observation, like an eagle hovering high in the sky, observing all that is below. This is the ability to observe both our inner and outer worlds and the ability to express what we experience in our inner world.

This is masculine energy, which is associated with precision, logic and the courage to express one's inner truth and live by it. Through the throat centre we succeed in expressing ourselves freely, with a clear, strong and confident voice. Our inner voice guides us to our purpose. Through this chakra we learn to understand the deep meaning of the world and the true intentions of the people around us. We can learn about ourselves and the energetic states of the other chakras. The tone of our speech, its intonation and our body language are gateways through which our worldview passes. For example, we can examine how we say a seemingly simple sentence at dinner: "Please pass me the salt." The sentence can be said as a command, in a strong tone indicating anger and control; in a low, helpless voice pointing to insecurity; or in a clear, stable, balanced voice. The throat centre helps us actualize ourselves in the world and realize our full potential.

In the Bible it is written that God created the world through sound: "And God said: Let there be light. And there was light" (Genesis, 1:3). The idea that sounds create worlds exists in all cultures of the world. According to the Hindu belief, the world was created through the sound "Om". According to the Kabbalah, the sounds of the shofar (ram's horn) blown on Yom Kippur, the Day of Atonement, open the gates of heaven and change energetic fields. The spiral flow of air and sound going through the length of the ram's horn is an indicator of the spiral flow of the life force of the universe. Blowing the ram's horn is similar to the function of prayer during Rosh Hashanah, the Jewish New Year: it cleanses and purifies the negative energies that have clung to us during the past year.

We must watch the words we choose to speak. We must be precise with our intentions and energy and choose the appropriate word. We must focus our voice and speak with an intonation that expresses our intention in the clearest and best way. We must not misuse words, since words create reality. We must aspire to create the best and most beneficial reality we possibly can. The Throat Chakra teaches us to make requests, to say thank you, to ask for forgiveness and to give deserved praise with empowering words. We are all magicians, for good or bad, with an ability to cast spells or undo spells with words. We should avoid the use of negative words with regards to ourselves and others. We should use words to express love and gratitude. Say words of blessing, forgiveness, praise, constructiveness and creativity. Use positive words like: beautiful, wonderful, yes, of course, lovely, great, excellent, worthwhile, gladly. Say to yourself throughout the day: I look great, I am beautiful, I have energy, I'm smart, I'm successful, I'm wonderful, I love myself.

To prepare ourselves for drawing this mandala, we should pay attention to our speech for a few days. Note what we express out loud and what we cover up and hide. What words do we use? Do the words express a clear or unclear message? Is it easier for us to be silent with others or to speak fluently? What intonations do we use? From where does our voice originate – from our stomach or throat? Do we feel that we express ourselves clearly? Which is it easier for us to express, feelings of love or anger?

The template for the Throat Chakra is based on the triangle and the number three, which are energies of masculinity and precision. The triangle represents our ability to direct the energy according to our path. The number three represents knowledge and truth. Drawing the mandala releases obstacles that block self-expression and helps us listen to our inner voice, empower it with courage, connect to our inner truth and express it in our daily reality.

Throat Chakra Meditation

Sit in a comfortable position on a chair or pillow; make sure your spine is erect but relaxed. Imagine a ring connected to a taut string at the crown of your head pulling your spine upward, creating space, letting your lungs open wide. Close your eyes and focus on your breathing. Air enters, air exits. With each exhale, release all the tension in your body. Take seven deep breaths. Concentrate on the air that enters and exits your body. Tightly tense the muscles of your eyes, lips, shoulders, arms, hands, buttocks, abdomen, legs and feet. Then relax each body part, one after the other. Repeat this tensing and relaxing.

Inhale and then exhale, saying the sound "Om" out loud. In Eastern cultures, Om is considered the first sound according to which the universe was created, and it creates within us a connection to the world's frequency. Repeat the sound "Om" three times. While focusing within, say out loud the first authentic sound that comes to you. This sound can be expressed in song, in melody or gibberish, in whispers, shouts, or rising and falling tones, in laughter or crying. Continue to express these sounds as you breathe for about ten minutes.

Slowly and gently open your eyes. With inspiration from the sounds you vocalized, draw your mandala.

HOW TO DRAW THE MANDALA

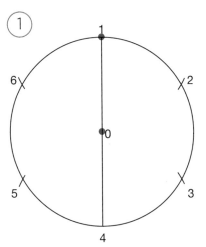

1 Open the compass to a radius of 9cm (3½in) and draw a circle. Place the compass point on the top of the circle at point 1. Using the same radius, divide the circle into six equal parts. Mark points 2 through 6.

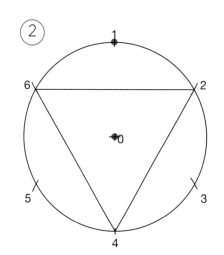

2 Connect the triangle between points 6, 2 and 4.

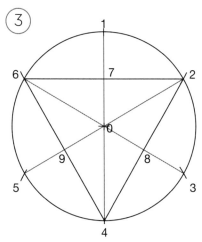

3 Place a ruler between points 1 and 4 and mark point 7 on line 6–2. Place the ruler between points 6 and 3 and mark point 8 on line 4–2. Place the ruler between points 2 and 5, mark point 9 on line 6–4.

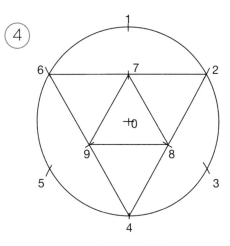

4 Connect the triangle between points 9, 8 and 7.

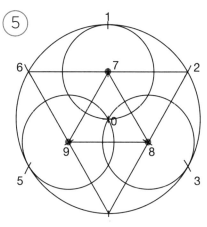

5 Place the point of the compass at point 7, adjust the radius to the size of segment 1–7 and draw a circle. Draw circles of the same size radius at points 8 and 9.

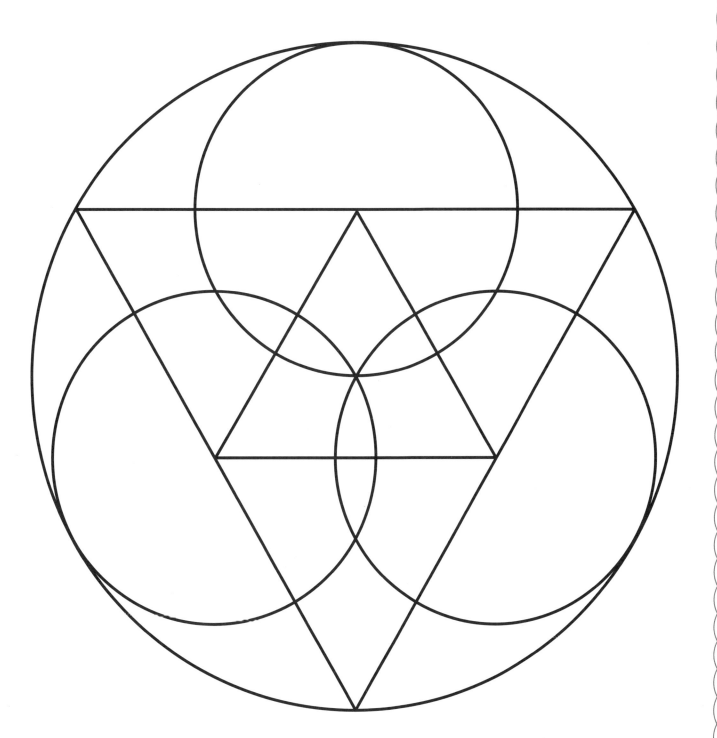

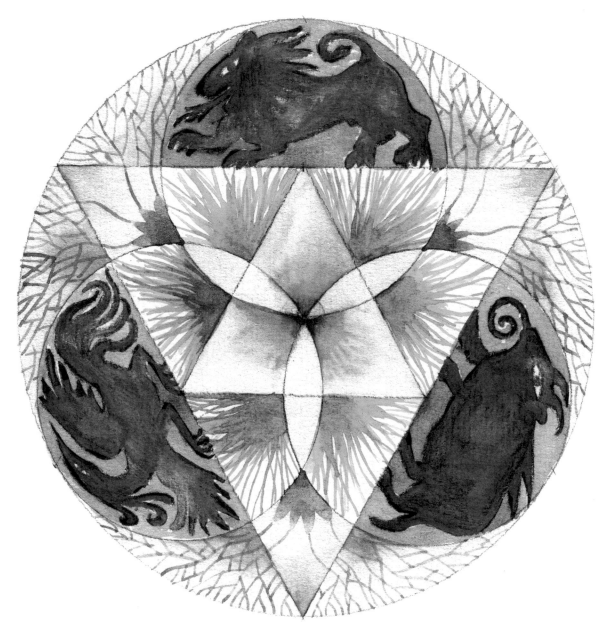

The lion, the eagle and the bull are the three powers of creation. The lion represents the fire element and symbolizes the energy and passion to create. The eagle represents the air element and symbolizes the power of imagination which is the source of ideas. And the bull represents the earth element, symbolizing the manifestation of creation in the material world. In the centre of the mandala is the creation, flowing and free.

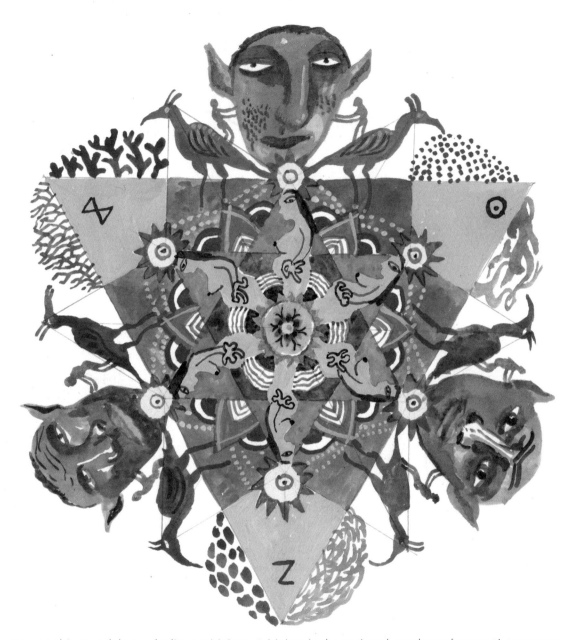

For me this mandala symbolizes criticism. Criticism is the major obstacle to the creative process. Three demons look from afar with discerning, critical eyes. In the centre of the mandala, women, exposed and submissive, move in a circle. When I look at this mandala I can see the forces within me that prevent my creative expression from flowing freely.

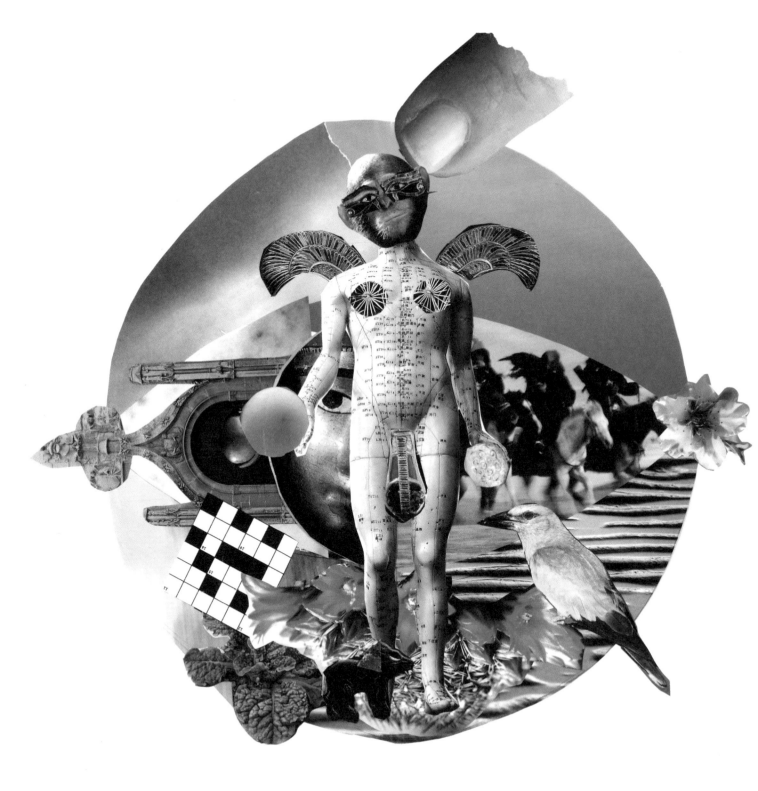

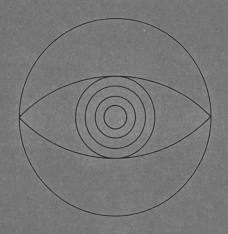

15

THIRD EYE CHAKRA MANDALA
ON THE WINGS OF IMAGINATION

To what extent does intuition light my path?
Can I rely on my imagination?
What is my relationship with the dark side within me?

The History of the Third Eye Chakra Meditation

The colour of the Third Eye Chakra is violet or indigo, the colour of the unconscious. This chakra is located between the two eyebrows. In Hinduism and Buddhism, the third eye is a symbol of enlightenment. This is the centre of thought, imagination, the mysterious and the unconscious. Its function is to connect us to our sixth sense and to the world beyond. Using the imagination we can perceive truths that belong to the concealed world and discover knowledge hidden within us, in our unconscious. The third eye connects to feminine energy: energy of the night, of dreams, of intuition and of a broad view of reality. Using the third eye it is possible to connect to the true essence of things. We receive messages through our five senses, but the third eye gives them a deeper meaning. It enables us to see reality from a different and broader perspective while staying ready, alert and open to receiving messages. Using the third eye is a learning process which requires quieting one's inner noise, openness, concentration and deep listening to knowledge that has been passed down through ancient traditions.

The third eye is the centre of supernatural and highly intuitive powers, the sixth sense. Through this chakra one can receive guidance, channelled messages and a connection to the higher self. This is the centre that enables telepathic experiences, astral journeys, past life recall, communication with the unconscious and intuition. Through the third eye we begin to channel, receive various messages from other worlds and other times – past, present and future, and from faraway places that the human eye has never seen. From this place we begin to see how we create our reality. This ability of discernment is what makes it possible for a person to fulfill their life not only according to what they want, but also according to what the universe wants, which becomes what they want.

All knowledge exists in the universe; the ability to receive this knowledge is conditional on a person's ability to connect to these sources of knowledge. The Third Eye Chakra enables us to connect to extrasensory perception, dreams, meditations and visions, the ability to see entities, auras and inside objects and bodies. Throughout history there have been a variety of methods used to see that which is concealed. For example, the priests in Babel "read" animal entrails and, in Greece, suppliants and seekers of truth consulted the Oracle of Delphi.

In the world, different methods of prophesizing and visualization developed related to the ability to see the concealed, the province of the Sixth Chakra. Some are well-known, like tarot cards and astrology, and some are less known, such as Tibetan predictions using fortune cookies. There are those who can see the future in a person's face or hand or foot. There are methods for making predictions using the Old Testament, clouds, coffee grinds or tea leaves left in a cup. Other methods use a crystal ball, sand or water, oil or wax in a bowl of water, salt, lit candles, smoke, the reflection of the moon in a mirror, a pendulum moving from side to side in different directions and more.

We shall work on the Third Eye Chakra mandala inspired by the words of the noted French author Antoine de Saint Exupéry in his book *The Little Prince*: "Behind everything that can be seen is something greater. Everything is a path, a gate or a window that opens to something else". Working with techniques such as collage or diluted watercolours stimulates the imagination and creativity. Through the mandala we expand our inner vision of things. We can understand the world through messages sent to us from the divine treasure hidden in the depths of the soul.

We will spread the wings of our imagination using the collage technique. Collage is a seemingly random juxtaposition of scraps of various pictures that receive new meaning when placed in a composition. Interpreting the collage lets us receive messages from our unconscious. To create a collage, gather magazines, postcards, pictures from old books, etc., on a variety of subjects: travel, fashion, art, nature – anything that can be torn and recycled. Working intuitively, cut or tear images from the materials you have gathered and paste them onto the template drawn according to the instructions below.

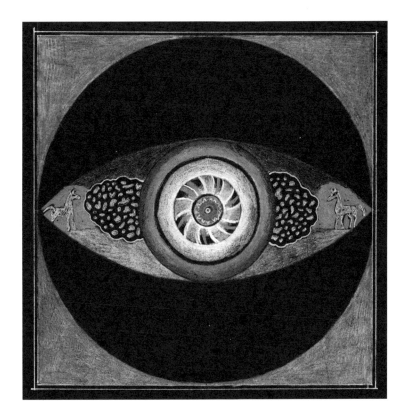

Third Eye Chakra Meditation

Sit in a comfortable position on a chair or pillow; make sure your spine is erect but relaxed. Imagine a ring connected to a taut string at the crown of your head pulling your spine upward, creating space, letting your lungs open wide. Close your eyes and focus on your breathing. Air enters, air exits. With each exhale, release all the tension in your body. Take seven deep breaths. Concentrate on the air that enters and exits your body. Tightly tense the muscles of your eyes, lips, shoulders, arms, hands, buttocks, abdomen, legs and feet. Then relax each body part, one after the other. Repeat this tensing and relaxing.

Using a white cup, prepare a cup of coffee or tea that causes grounds or leaves to remain in the bottom of the cup. After you finish drinking, turn the cup over on a plate. Then turn it back, right side up. Unique shapes will have formed on the sides of the cup. Looking carefully, and using your imagination, these coffee grounds (or tea leaves) will turn into clear, strong images. Write down the images, sights and stories that you see. These images bring us messages like the visions and archetypes in a dream.

In this atmosphere of intuitive contemplation, begin to work on the mandala using the collage technique.

HOW TO DRAW THE MANDALA

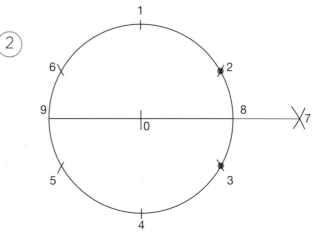

Open the compass to a radius of 8cm (3in) and draw a circle. Place the compass point at the top of the circle, point 1, and divide the circle into six equal parts using the circle's radius. Mark points 2–6.

Place the compass point at point 2 and mark a small arc opposite the centre (point 0). Place the compass point at point 3 and intersect the arc with another arc and mark it point 7. Place a ruler between points 7 and 0 and draw line 8–9.

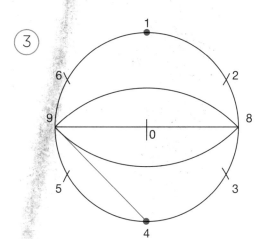

③ Place the compass point at point 4 and increase the radius size to that of segment 4–9. With the compass point still at point 4, draw the upper arc 8–9. Place the compass point at point 1 and draw the lower arc 8–9.

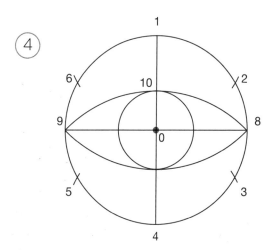

④ Place the ruler between points 1 and 4 and mark point 10 on the upper arc. Place the compass point at point 0 and decrease the radius size to the length of the segment 0–10. Draw a circle with this radius.

⑤ At the right intersection of the circle with line 8–9, mark point A. With a radius of the length of the segment 0–10, place the compass at point A and mark point B on the circle above and point C on the circle below.

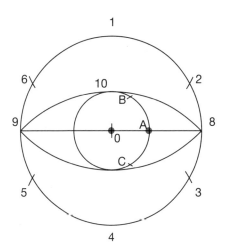

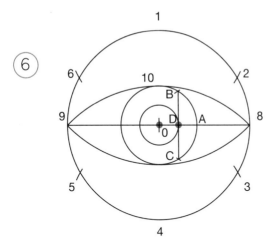

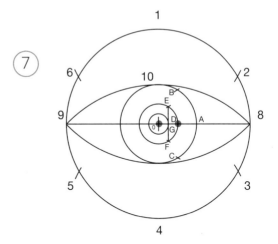

Place the ruler between points B and C and mark the point of intersection on line 8–9 (point D). Place the compass at point 0 and draw a circle with a radius of 0–D.

Place the compass at point D and, with the radius of 0–D, mark points E above and F below on the circle. Place the ruler between points E and F and mark the point G on line 8–9. Place the compass at point 0 and draw a circle with a radius of 0–G.

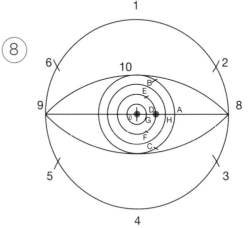

Place the compass at point D and mark point H on line 8–9. Place the compass at point 0 and draw a circle with a radius of 0–H.

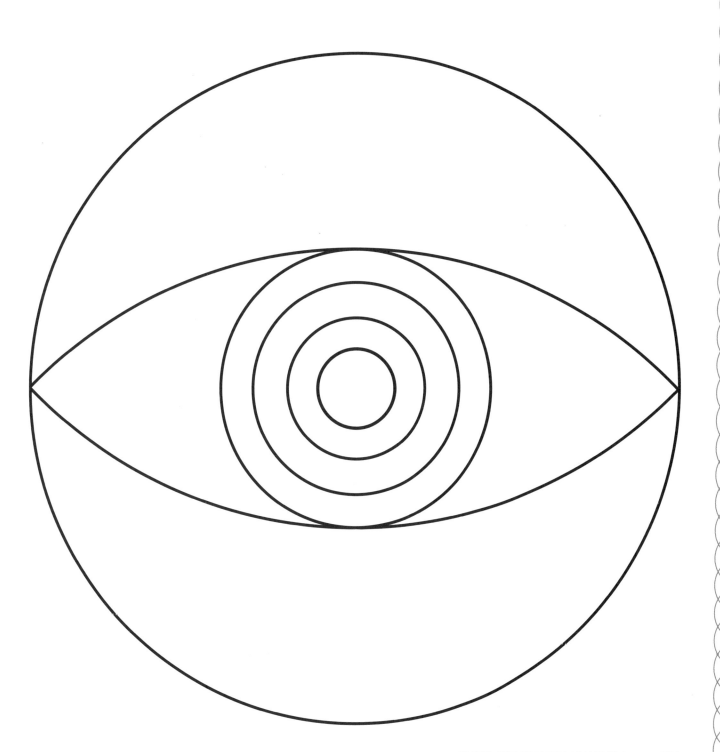

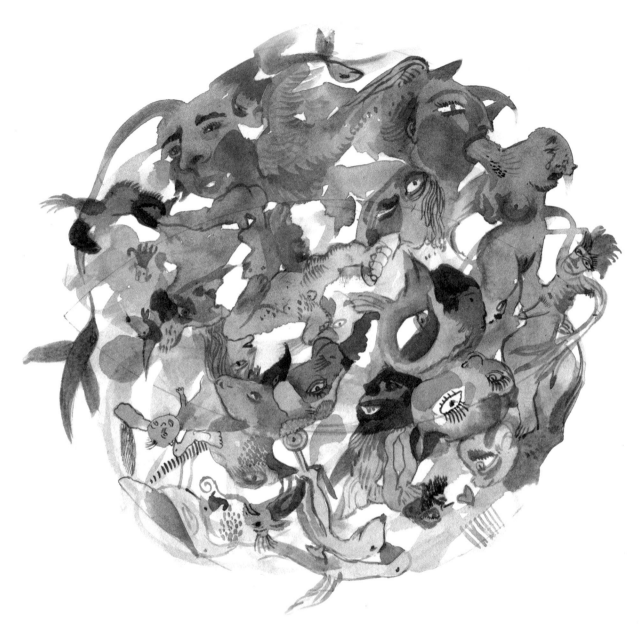

I painted freely with watercolours on the template. After they dried I looked for images within the blotches, like interpreting Rorschach inkblots. Thus I allowed the voice of my inner imagination free rein. Slowly, strange images and imaginary shapes appeared. I contemplated them and gave them names and stories; I tried to learn what they aroused in me.

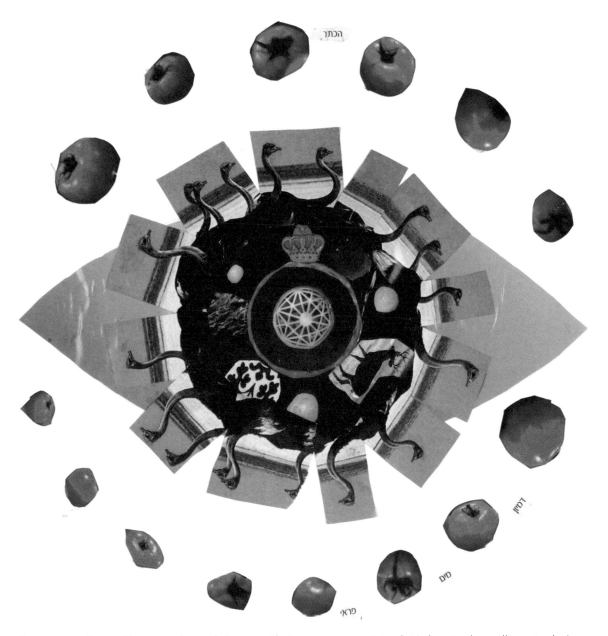

The unconscious talks to us through images that we are meant to decipher. In the collage technique, images become riddles. I wonder what red tomatoes mean – flirtatiousness and sensuality? Why are they in the outer circle? Why did I paste a shape with clear, straight lines in the centre of the mandala? What things am I hiding in the sand like an ostrich?

THIRD EYE CHAKRA MANDALA   189

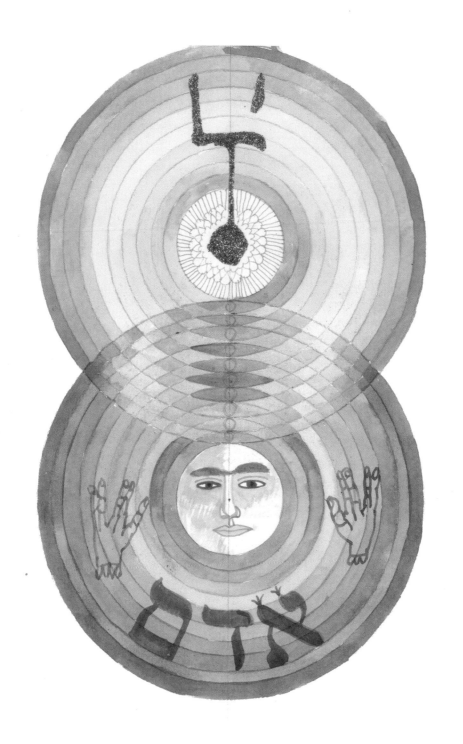

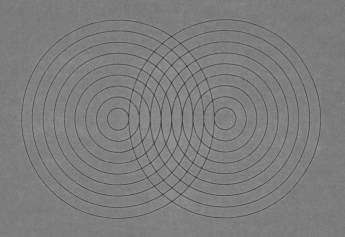

16

CROWN CHAKRA MANDALA
IN HIS IMAGE

How can I connect to the divine essence within me?
Am I fulfilling my life's purpose?
What is the meaning of life and death?

The History of the Crown Chakra Mandala

The Seventh Chakra, located at the crown of the head, is our connection to the infinite. Its colour is white or gold. According to Hindu symbolism, the Crown Chakra is represented by a lotus flower of 1,000 petals. The Crown Chakra is the last chakra on our journey up the ladder of chakras. It is our connection to divine knowledge. It represents the source, the place from which everything comes and to which everything returns. It is like a drop of water in the ocean: the drop contains all the elements of the ocean and when the drop returns to the ocean it merges with it completely. At the beginning of our journey in a human body, we separate from the source and receive a separate identity. After we have fulfilled our purpose on earth, we are ready to continue on the path of souls, through the gate of death found in the Crown Chakra.

We contain all knowledge within us, which makes it possible to know the world through inner contemplation. The gateway to the universe is the Crown Chakra, which enables us to connect to cosmic knowledge. The seventh centre is the spiritual centre through which we experience God's manifestations in the world. We understand that all creatures are part of and come from the divine essence and that humans are part of this unity. Our relationship to cosmic energy comes from love and devotion. The divine does not control us but rather guides and directs us on the paths of life. According to Buddhism, we can choose to connect to the divine source and aspire to happiness and enlightenment. In this way we trust and believe that we have a purpose to fulfil and it is for this purpose that we came into the world.

According to Buddhist beliefs, all people are caught up in the Wheel of Samsara: a recurring cycle of birth, life, death and then rebirth. Through learning, contemplation and intention, we have the possibility of becoming enlightened, leaving Samsara and attaining Nirvana – a place of infinite bliss. In order to open the Crown Chakra, it is necessary to do inner work that helps us approach the divine, such as developing humility, compassion and connecting to truth and unlimited, unconditional love. In all religions and beliefs this is done through prayer, practice and meditation. The meaning of the colour white is purity. This is the colour that contains all the other colours within it. The meaning of the colour gold is the connection to the higher self. Through the Crown Chakra we receive the frequencies of all the colours united in one ray of light. The refraction of the light ray into the seven colours of the chakras is its human embodiment in this world

Etty Hillesum was a Jewish woman from Amsterdam whose life was cut short at the age of 29 in the Nazi death camps. She wrote a diary between 1941 and 1942 describing her spiritual journey and encounter with the divine within: "Every day I get new strength from the spring of springs, from life itself, and from time to time I rest in prayer ... whoever goes through the long, arduous and neverending process and reaches the source of power within himself, that I want to call God, and whoever takes care that the path to God remains open ... continually draws new strength from the same source" (*The Sky Within Me*, 28 September 1943).

Rabbi Nachman from Breslav teaches that going into nature alone at night is a way to experience unification with the divine essence: "Know that the most important aspect of nullification of the ego (bitul) – that a person casts off his being and becomes void, and becomes part of the unity of God, blessed be He – occurs only in self-imposed solitude. And the solitude needs a special time and place so that obstacles do not confuse him. Night is the time; awaken at night when everything else is asleep. And the place is on a lone path, not the road of the many, where passersby may stop you; rather, do not walk the road of the many but on the road that few walk. Go and find solitude ... and then, when we completely nullify ourselves, one can be joined in unity with God, blessed be He ... "

The template for the Crown Chakra mandala is constructed from the intersection of two circles. The two circles together form the symbol of infinity, or a number eight that is "lying down" on its side, like a Moebius Ring, a strip that is given a half-twist, and then joined at the ends to form a loop so that the outside and the inside form a continuous surface. One side symbolizes the divine, and the other, the human. Thus the soul passes from this world to the world beyond.

Crown Chakra Meditation

Sit in a comfortable position on a chair or pillow; make sure your spine is erect but relaxed. Imagine a ring connected to a taut string at the crown of your head pulling your spine upward, creating space, letting your lungs open wide. Close your eyes and focus on your breathing. Air enters, air exits. With each exhale, release all the tension in your body. Take seven deep breaths. Concentrate on the air that enters and exits your body. Tightly tense the muscles of your eyes, lips, shoulders, arms, hands, buttocks, abdomen, legs and feet. Then relax each body part, one after the other.

Repeat this tensing and relaxing.

Using your imagination, envision a horizontal number eight formed by a white, radiant light. This is the symbol of infinity. The left side represents our manifestation in the world, and the right side symbolizes the divine source. Imagine yourself walking on the path formed by this figure eight a number of times. The point of connection between the two sides – which is the centre of infinity – is the bindu point. According to the Kabbalah, this is the point of divine contraction (tzimtzum) by way of which the world was created.

As you experience a feeling of oneness with the source, open your eyes and begin to draw the mandala.

HOW TO DRAW THE MANDALA

① Draw a horizontal line 30cm (12in) in the centre of the page and mark the centre of the line as point 6. Mark five points at a distance of 1cm (½in) from each other to the right and to the left of point 6, and number them from 1–5 and 7–11.

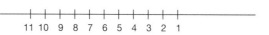

② Place the point of the compass at point 1 and draw a circle with a radius of 1–2. Place the point of the compass at point 11 and draw a circle with the same radius. Place the compass point again at point 1 and draw a circle with a radius of 1–3. Place the point of the compass at point 11 and draw a circle with the same radius.

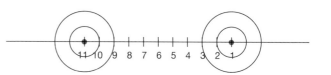

③ Continue in this manner to draw the rest of the circles.

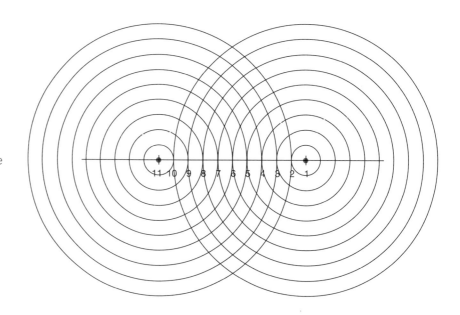

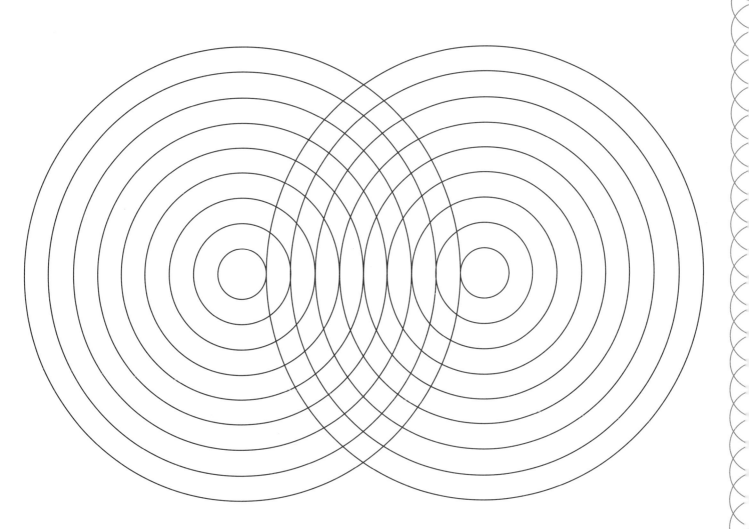

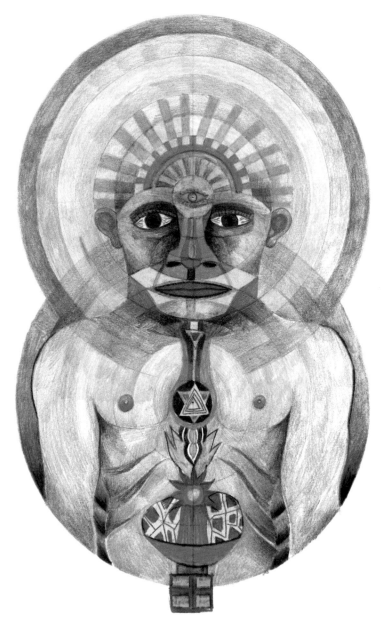

For me, this mandala represents the connection between God and humanity. The two circles intertwined with one another are like the connection of humanity with our Creator. The upper circle represents the divine spirit and in its centre is the third eye that connects us to the worlds of the spirit. The lower circle represents the body and human emotions, whose centre is the heart through which we sense the world.

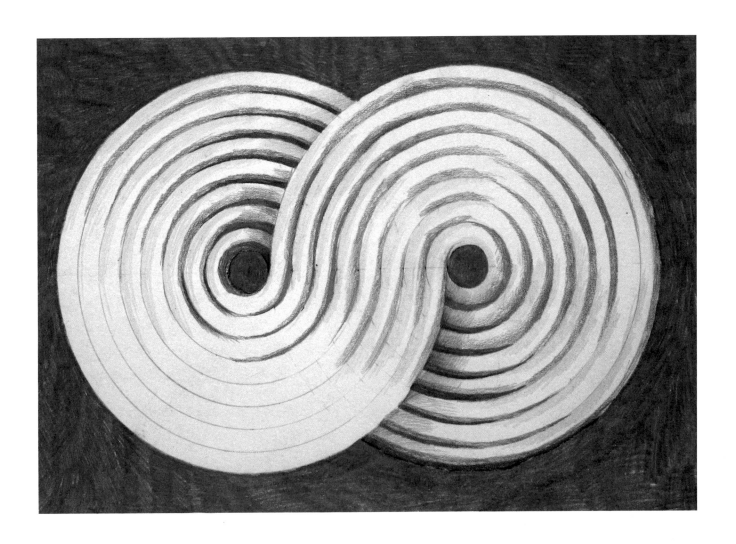

The mandala template creates the symbol and movement of infinity. For me, the number eight represents the idea that our souls go through repeated incarnations of death and rebirth.

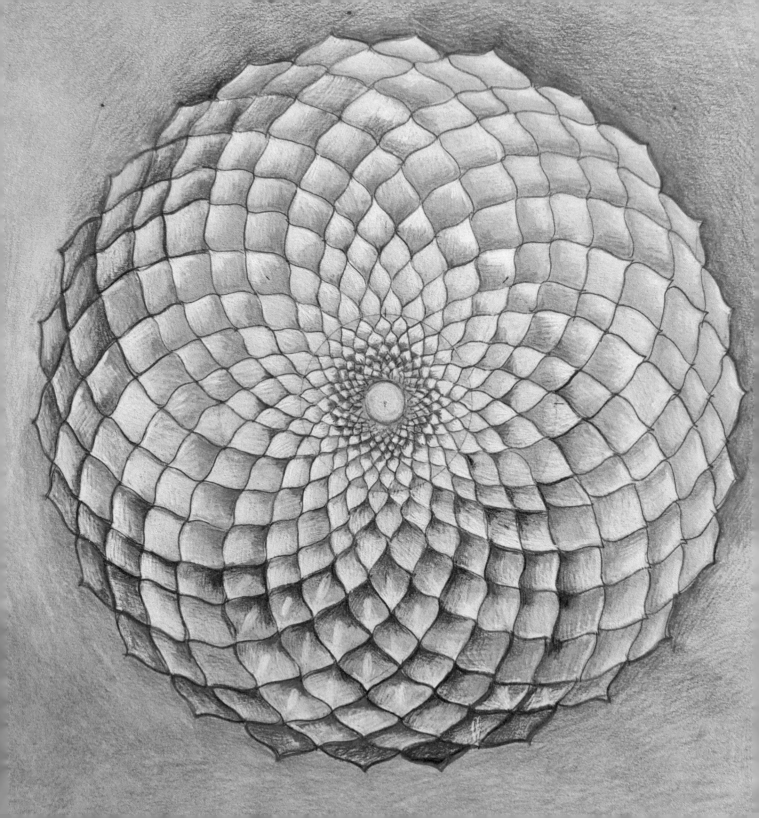

EPILOGUE

This book was written to get to know the spiritual practice of mandala paintings from a closer and more intimate perspective, to create a special tool that will allow us to pause for a moment in the race of life and focus our attention on the inner world. It is easy for us to listen to the needs of others and to focus on our chores and duties in daily life, but when we draw a mandala, we take the time to connect with our feelings, thoughts, imagination and bodily sensations. Peace and quiet make it possible to discover the inner point, the bindu, where our true essence lies. The connection to the bindu makes it possible to feel that life moves from moment to moment, here and now, without fear of the future or longing for the past. This way we can float across the river of life and let the forces of nature propel us as we observe and enjoy the changing sights we encounter along the way.

Through mandala paintings we can live in harmony and satisfaction with what we have, without seeking approval from the outside world. Fame, wealth, success, medals and certificates of honour will no longer be our priorities; they will be replaced by an attitude of love and respect for who we are, even if we are not whole or complete. In a wonderful way we can feel more whole than ever before.

Mandala paintings help us to make space and time for our creative expression. Through creation we explore and better understand the essence of life and its meaning. As we deepen and establish our ability to act from our central point, we are able to feel waves of abundance flowing from the hidden depths of the soul. We learn to listen to guidelines that make our decisions precise. Our intuition guides us to the next step we must take in the journey of life. A rainbow of shades opens up for us into a fan of options we have never seen before

When we draw mandalas consistently, at least two or three times a week, our contemplation of life expands to new dimensions we have not yet experienced. Our attitude toward others becomes more forgiving, compassionate and loving. We understand that others are our mirror, and that each of the people we meet is one of thousands of reflections of the infinite soul within us.

Painting the mandala encourages us to live without struggles or conflicts. Our soul wishes to connect in unity with the collective soul of all the people in the world. Every person has the hidden potential to be an artist in their own unique way, if only we could avoid judgement, listening to and accepting people's heartfelt feelings. The mandala is meant to connect us to each other, knowing that there is no good or bad artist; we are all souls seeking to express our inner truth, and we must support each other so that we can fulfil this wish. In the new world we are building, there is no room for competition and criticism but only support, encouragement and love for every creator.

I pray that the painting of the mandala will bring love, peace, quiet and harmony to the world.

Amen.

ABOUT THE AUTHOR

Eitan Kedmy is a mandala artist who teaches others how to draw and paint mandala art as a way to develop personal and spiritual growth.

He began painting at a very early age – in fact, he has no memories of himself without a pintbrush in his hand. Ever since, his life has been filled with art.

Eitan studied Visual Communications at the Bezalel Academy of Arts and Design in Jerusalem. After graduating, he opened his own graphic design and illustration company in Tel Aviv. For more than 20 years he designed logos, illustrated children's books, created cartoons for newspapers and taught drawing and graphic design.

In his spare time, he would spend time in his studio painting large acrylic works on canvas. Eventually, he shifted focus and opened his own ceramics studio. For seven years he created clay sculptures. He has also contributed to many drawing, sculpture and illustration exhibitions in various museums and galleries in Israel.

He was first introduced to mandalas at a birthday party with his daughters. Since then, he has been an enthusiastic mandala artist. mandala filled his life with colour, emotion, serenity and a new understanding of reality.

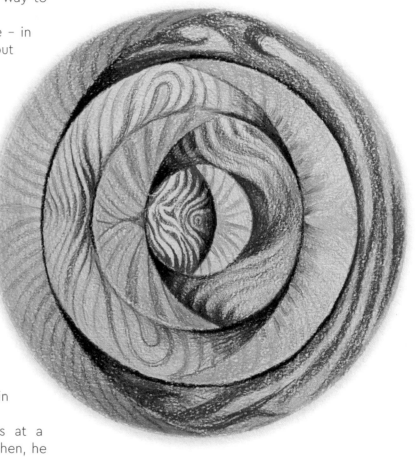